Nimbus Publishing Limited
P.O. Box 9301, Station A
Halifax, NS B3K 5N5
(902) 455-4286

Editing and design: Nancy Roberts Design
Printed and bound in Canada

Canadian Cataloguing in Publication Data
Aikens, Gwladys M. Rees (Gwladys May Rees), 1916–
Nurses in battledress
2nd ed.
ISBN 1-55109-313-8

1. Aikens, Gwladys M. Rees (Gwladys May Rees), 1916–
2. Great Britain. Army. Queen Alexandra's Imperial Military Nursing Service/Reserve -- Biography.
3. World War, 1939–1945 -- Personal narratives, British.
4. World War, 1939–1945 -- Medical care -- Great Britain.
I. Title.

D811.5.A37 1999 940.54'7541'092 C99-950137-2

Nimbus Publishing acknowledges the financial support of the Canada Council and the Department of Canadian Heritage

Acknowledgements

My daughter, Patricia M. Aikens, for putting together the original book for the family in 1994

My sons David, Douglas and Geoffrey for faith and support

Eva Munro and Julie Ross for making things happen

Graham McBride of the Maritime Museum of the Atlantic, Halifax, NS, for the photograph of the Strathallan and for vital information on the Bari Raid of 1943

Friends too numerous to name for their encouragement

To the memory of
my beloved husband Robert L. Aikens,
a native Nova Scotian

Contents

About the Queen Alexandra's Imperial Military Nursing Service

This nursing service was founded by Queen Alexandra, wife and widow of Edward VII, who took an interest in the care of the military sick and wounded. The "Q.As" comprise two distinct branches, the Regulars and the Reserves. Regulars used the full name above and the Reserves used the same with " /Reserve" added at the end, or alternatively, Q.A.I.M.N.S./R.

The Regulars were career military nurses who staffed permanent British military hospitals around the world in peacetime.

Q.A. Reserve units were formed only in wartime and their job was to perform the nursing care of soldiers en route from battleground casualty clearance stations to base hospital and in temporary base hospitals. Thus, they always went overseas and into war zones. Much acute care was required for serious wounds, and it was often given under arduous conditions.

While both Regulars and Reserves are called Q.A.s, this book is about Q.A. Reserves except in a few places where "Regular" is stated.

At the end of World War II, Queen Mary (widow of George V) presented the Nursing Mirror Trophy to the Q.A.I.M.N.S./R. at the Passing Out Parade in the grounds of Anstie Grange, Holmwood Surrey.

Author's Note

One knowledgeable publishing person has disliked my "detached" tone. I don't know how I could tell some of the events herein at all without detachment. Believe me, we felt them keenly at the time and I still do today.

One decision I made is related to the issue of detachment – except for certain incidents, I have not described the horrible wounds we treated continually. I want you to know about my experiences, but I do not wish for you to experience them vicariously.

When I describe shopping or mountain-climbing junkets, please be aware that these were encouraged, facilitated and sometimes required by our command to help keep us fit for our gruelling and heart-rending duties. Our medical reason for being was foremost in our lives and thoughts, and our duties sometimes nearly overwhelmed us.

The veterans of World War II are quite old or already gone. I hope this book brings a few of the nurses or maybe their children out of the woodwork. I would so like to hear from you. Please write to the Nimbus Publishing address on page ii.

Gwladys M. Rees Aikens
August 1998

Preface

This book has had as complicated a journey as my own journeys in World War II. Here is an outline of the book's journey.

1946 I arrived in Canada, a war bride, on the Queen Mary, which landed us at Pier 21, Halifax.

1947 Robert and I lived in Montreal while Robert studied for and passed his Fellowship exams in medicine. I had accepted a position at the Shriners Hospital.

I was interviewed by the CBC because of my war experiences and probably because I, along with 80-odd others, had shared a lifeboat with Margaret Bourke-White, the Life Magazine photographer. The interviewer said I should write a book.

I had never seen the Bourke-White photos and article about the sinking of the Strathallan, but at this point I wrote to her and received a nice letter and the Life Magazine pages containing her article, which I still have.

I also wrote the British War Office and received detailed notes on the operations surrounding rescue of Strathallan passengers and the attempts to salvage the ship. I was pleased to note that in the end most people had been rescued, although there was nothing in particular about nurses, the girl with the broken leg or other individuals whose exact fate I never will know.

1948–49 Arrived in Halifax to a very busy medical life and eventually four children. No time for book writing, but I did start to collect bits and pieces, snaps, dates, the usual World War II memorabilia.

1968 Robert was about to present papers on sarcoidosis and pneumoconiosis in Wales and Germany. Thinking of writing a book on this as well as the war sometime. In the future.

I would accompany him and while in London I would get some information I needed for the book about the Bari Raid in Italy, which for some reason seemed difficult to obtain by mail. By mail I got the impression that the authorities thought that the event had never happened, which is how they had acted at the time.

Two weeks before we were to leave, Robert went to hospital with his first heart attack and someone gave his papers in his place. Robert died in 1972.

1980–90 The book was dropped until 1980, when I decided it should be put together. By this time my children, who had grown up with the idea that their parents were going to write their book on World War II, were old enough to see the need for preserving their mother's (and father's) story while it still could be recaptured. It was definitely a story my family and friends wanted to read.

The collection of "pieces" started once more, and the problem of the Bari Raid resumed exactly where it had left off. Such had been the secrecy that when Robert had come over to Italy from North Africa in 1944, only months after, he had not heard of it. Even though he was a medical officer and part of its horror was huge medical problems we could not handle satisfactorily.

1993–94 I decided to go ahead with my book without confirmation of the Bari Raid. Having come to Canada and with years gone by, I was no longer in contact with anyone else who had been there. I had no source whatever of confirmation of this searing experience. A book was written and copyrighted and four copies were bound for my four children after intense labour by my daughter Patricia to type and organize the manuscript from tapes.

1995 Purely by chance I obtained the information I needed, not from the War Office in London, but here in Halifax through the Maritime Museum of the Atlantic. I had asked for a photo of the Strathallan, my convoy ship, from the Museum's excellent archives, had mentioned the Bari Raid as an ongoing difficulty in my project, and Graham McBride soon after sent me the magazine article about the Bari Raid. Apparently the information had only recently been released.

On holiday in Corfu with my oldest son and family, we arranged to ferry to Bari, Italy, for a day visit. [See Epilogue, Return to Bari.] Where there should have been far over 1000 graves of casualties of the Bari Raid (military casualties alone), there was only one marker in the military cemetery for the time period in question. Without the magazine article, I would have doubted my sanity at this point.

1996–97 Information from the UK indicated that there were few or maybe no books on the Q.A.s in World War II. I had met a woman Canadian veteran who was campaigning for greater recognition of women's role in World War II in the form of monuments.

1998 I do not particularly agree with monuments, but I decided that my book would not have done its entire job unless I published it – then there would be at least one full account in the world of a Q.A.'s service and of those who served with her. I knew it had to be done, and done by me, even though I had never put out a book before and couldn't really afford it, as a sort of memorial for both sides of the Atlantic.

HOW IS IT POSSIBLE that more than fifty years have passed since World War II threw Bob and me together? Sometimes the memories are unleashed without warning, precipitated by something as seemingly insignificant as the aroma of welsh cakes cooking on the griddle or the arc of steaming tea filling a fragile china cup. Sometimes it means just a sigh and returning to the moment's preoccupation, but often it means taking a moment to reflect.

The pages of our albums are faded, worn and ear-marked from thumbing through, and many of the photo corners are missing so that the snaps peer out lopsidedly from the pages. There is Bob with the Major and a few of the other uniformed men, and there I am in my grey and scarlet Q.A. uniform with white headdress, a hand up to shade my eyes from the sun. There's another snap of the gang, the names of whom elude me now.

Like little rockets, these pictures catapult me back to the desert, back to North Africa, back in time to England and to Wales, the place of my birth.

U.K.

1941

Preparation for War

When Britain declared war on Germany in 1939, I was just completing my hospital training. In 1934, after two years of college in my home town of Swansea, south Wales, I had completed two years of training in the King Edward VII Childrens' Orthopaedic Hospital, Rivelin Valley in Sheffield, England. This was followed by three years of general training in a large general hospital in Sheffield, and then eighteen months of midwifery training. I completed my SRN, or State Registered Nurse, exams in 1939 and, in early 1941, had successfully passed my exam to become a state certified midwife.

World War II was well advanced by the time I volunteered for active service in 1941. The final part of my hospital training was accomplished under the most hazardous of conditions during the Battle of Britain, which had begun in June of 1940 and would stretch out until April 1941. The hospital complex in which I was working comprised a large general hospital with 1000 beds, together with a midwifery training centre and midwifery hospital with about 200 beds. Windows had been covered with thick black strapping tape, and all studies and work were performed under the eerie glow of lights covered with blue paper. There was to be no light showing out of doors.

We had been meticulously trained for all eventualities in both medical and war-related matters. One threat which we thought we might have to contend with was a poisonous gas attack. When outdoors, we wore gas masks strung around our necks.

As our superiors wanted to ensure their medical staff had the best possible protection, our gas masks and the people wearing them were put to the ultimate test. We were shunted through gas mask vans, which were large, sealed, buslike vehicles inside of which supposedly three or four types of poisonous gases were released. Heaven only knows if they used the real thing, but none of us died from the sheer terror of being herded into that enclosed space and exposed to the frightening gases inside.

In anticipation of gas attacks, some of our hospital wards had been set up specifically for gas casualties. However, I didn't experience the horror of gas casualties until much later in my war service. I was on call for duty on that ward and, as all hospital staff were housed within in the hospital, if on call we could reach the ward at a moment's notice. And we seemed to be on call constantly, 24 hours a day, really, because we were always on the alert for a blitz – a lightning-fast enemy attack by air.

Barrage balloons in the sky added another element to the state of readiness for war. These were huge, cylindrical hot air balloons anchored in the sky so that they formed a sort of barrier to prevent enemy planes from flying low over their targets. On the ground below were soldiers armed with "ack-ack," or antiaircraft, guns ready to attack any enemy plane daring to penetrate the barrier.

In different ways we were discovering what sorts of things had already been happening in this war. A small paperback book called *Dachau* circulated at the hospital and was read with horror by the staff. Some refugee nurses from Czechoslovakia who worked with us related the atrocities being committed on the Continent. We listened, incredulous, scarcely able to believe what we were hearing.

Air-raid shelters were being hastily constructed throughout the city of Sheffield. We had become well accustomed to the drone of planes overhead. Since the onset of the war we had heard our Royal Air Force squadrons flying above us in the daytime and always wondered where they were headed. Two friends of the family, boys I had grown up with who had become Spitfire pilots, had been shot down, one of them over the North Sea and the other in Cologne. Both were missing and presumed dead.

As we didn't have access to television at that time, we got information from friends and relatives, listened intently to the daily radio news and watched Pathe Gazette newsreel at the cinema so that we could keep abreast of the situation at home and abroad.

Britain never knew which city would be targeted by the enemy as that night's bombing victim. One evening as we were checking patients on our ward, we heard the drone of enemy planes over the hospital and held our breath as they flew past. By now, we could distinguish friend from foe just by the sound above us. We learned later that those planes had bombed Coventry that night, flying right over Sheffield en route to their destination. They had spared us, at least for the moment.

Blitz on Sheffield

A blitz defies all description. How the constantly-attacked cities of London and Coventry endured the incessant bombing I will never know. That first blitz on Sheffield is still clearly ingrained in my mind. The hospital was on the outskirts of Sheffield, and, as it was my day off, I decided to accompany a friend into the city for lunch, shopping and a show. After treating ourselves to a light lunch and traipsing around to a number of shops, we headed for a local tearoom where we consumed cups of aromatic tea and numerous jam- and cream-laden scones.

Now, much later, we were scanning the billboard outside the theatre deciding which show to see. For some reason, there seemed to prevail an air of uneasy expectancy around us; the city appeared devoid of passers-by and we wondered if perhaps we should just forget about the show and head back to our hospital residence. Our own planes hovered overhead as the inevitable searchlights scanned the buildings and streets of the city where dusk had now fallen.

For no logical reason we decided against staying to watch a show and instead headed off on foot in the direction of the hospital. No buses came by, so we continued walking, quickening our pace as if unseen forces were behind us urging us onward. And then the sirens signalled the enemy descent and we knew we had to beat a hasty retreat. An attack meant that we were needed in our places alongside the rest of the staff; everyone at our hospital would be on duty, day off or not.

My companion and I passed the large C&A, a department store sitting just on the fringe of the city shopping district. We knew the store's basement housed a spacious air-raid shelter, and we wondered if we should get in now before danger descended. But the shelter was full, apparently, and so we kept walking, briskly now, almost sprinting. We could see the flames of fires started by incendiaries, licking hungrily at the sooty skies in the distance behind us. Our nervousness intensified, our banter vanished, as we hurried on, heads down.

Now came the bombing – deafening thunderclap sounds, accompanied by brilliant flashes of light everywhere around us. We saw an enemy bomber falling like a comet from the sky, illuminating the department store over which it fell. Each time there was a ground-shaking explosion we ducked behind a hedge or large tree for protection. What sort of security we thought we would be getting from those objects, I'm not sure, but instinct dictated that we hide behind something. Through our haste and fright our slave-driven feet did their bidding, carrying us back to the hospital without so much as a scratch or blister.

As we were just about to scrub up for duty, we learned that the C&A Department Store shelter had received a direct hit; the shelter and its dead were just sealed up, finally. We witnessed the results of the blitz firsthand that night, as we were busier than ever, running back and forth among patients suffering the brunt of the air raid. Injured and dead were coming in from all areas. We could discern, through cracks in the doorways when they were opened and quickly shut again, enemy planes strafing the ambulances as they turned into the driveway of the hospital emergency building. Nothing was sacred in war, it seemed.

I was amazed to learn some days later that my name had been added to the list of missing persons posted on the city hall bulletin board. As soon as we could make contact with relatives, I let my mother know I was alive and well. She had, fortunately, heard only that a large city in the centre of England had been badly bombed and had assumed that it was Coventry again.

My friend and I had fled the city of Sheffield without seeing most of the damage. We knew that bombs had destroyed a lot of the city, but we couldn't have comprehended the damage before seeing it ourselves in the daylight. Now, as the two of us revisited the city centre a week after the devastation, we couldn't believe this picture of chaos and ruin was the same place. Many of the streets we had run through that night were now completely blockaded by rubble. Buildings had toppled, trees had been uprooted. We wondered how we had possibly managed to escape.

We also saw freak damage – houses with just one or two walls standing, pictures still hanging, though drunkenly, in place. A clock on one such lonely wall still ticked mechanically and showed the correct time. A stove was the solitary thing remaining in a house kitchen. There were no walls around it but a kettle and saucepan still sat on the burners where they'd been left. A woman passed us with a bundle of clothing and other belongings piled unsteadily in a rickety wheelbarrow. Atop the mound sat a little girl in a pretty party dress. Was this all they had left, I wondered. A man approached to help the woman. I wondered where they had lived and where they would live now.

A Sheffield newspaper reported, "Rescuers were still at work hours afterwards, seeking the missing among the debris. A number of houses were completely wrecked and many others damaged. Amid a pile of debris a dog lay on a bed and refused to be removed or to allow anyone near it with either food or water. From beneath another pile of debris an alarm clock rang."

Although I had seen pictures of war-shattered buildings in Europe, of devastation and grief, this was the closest I had come so far to experiencing the realities of war. Some of my friends had joined the armed forces, and the pictures of ruin printed indelibly on my brain had no trouble convincing me that I too was needed. Britain was badly in need of nurses overseas to care for the troops in the hospitals and I knew that I had the dedication and the training needed to help those who were fighting for the freedom of others. I was ready to join the army and help in the war effort.

Joining the Q.A. Reserves

After finishing my midwifery training in Sheffield, my friend Peggy Dickinson and I took temporary jobs as staff midwives at a hospital in Shoreham by the Sea near Brighton in the south of England. We then decided to make application to the Queen Alexandra's Imperial Military Nursing Service/Reserves. I wasn't sure of the origin of the name of the Q.A. Reserves although I believed that Queen Alexandra, the Danish wife of King Edward VII, had been interested in hospitals and nurses and probably had started this nursing service in World War I.

Britain had a standing army overseas and was therefore in need of staffed hospitals even in peacetime. In World War I, because Britain did not have enough regular nursing staff for all its army hospitals, it called up, from the British civilian hospitals, those nurses who had completed all their training. These nurses were referred to as the Q.A.I.M.N.S./R. or Q.A. Reserves.

The Q.A.I.M.N.S., or Q.A. Regulars, nurses permanently employed in British military hospitals throughout the British Empire, continued to staff military hospitals in peacetime and in countries where no war was raging. Q.A. Reserves were called up again in World War II to staff the hospitals in war zones.

The Reserve force was one of the elite nursing services staffing the military hospitals throughout the British Empire. The application form for entry into the Q.A. Reserves was a good indication of the qualifications required. An applicant had to be British, preferably English, with a good family background, finishing school or college and good social skills. Rules and regulations were spelled out precisely and it was made very clear that any violation of those rules would mean immediate dismissal and a return home without question.

The British Government had to assure itself of the loyalty of each individual entering the army and representing Britain overseas. They also wanted well adjusted people who would fit easily into any situation.

Thus, my first step was to travel to a military office in Brighton where I was subjected to a lengthy and rather complicated interview replete with hundreds of probing questions about my family, their occupations, my schooling, my extracurricular activities – Did I play tennis or some other sport? – and seemingly every other detail they could think of. Tennis?

I left mentally exhausted after sitting nervously upright in a hard wooden chair for this interview of over an hour, but I was confident that I would be offered the opportunity to serve as a member of the Queen Alexandra's Imperial Military Nursing Service, Reserve force.

Needing rest and relaxation after that gruelling parley, Peggy and I decided to take in a late-afternoon stage show featuring a young female singer named Vera Lynn. Her wavy blonde hair and svelte figure added the perfect touch to her stage charm, but it was her mystical, lilting voice that captivated us. We weren't to know at the time that Vera Lynn would become a household name in wartime Britain and would be known in many countries via radio and recordings.

The stage show helped to quell my nerves, but I needn't have worried because, as a result of a successful interview, I was accepted into the Q.A. Reserves and called up for military duty in July of 1942. Peggy Dickinson also joined, but I did not see her again until after the war.

Q.A. Military Duty – July and August 1942

My first five weeks of military duty were spent at Tidworth Military Hospital, a peacetime military base located on the Salisbury Plains in the south of England. I joined a number of other new nursing recruits who had been successful applicants to the Q.A. Reserves. Before beginning our nursing duties, we were given thorough medical examinations, including all the necessary inoculations for typhus, typhoid and smallpox.

Fully vaccinated and in certified good health, we still had to look our part. Austin Reed's, top-of-the-line London tailors, came to measure us for uniforms and we were soon outfitted in the distinctive grey and scarlet colours of the Q.A.s. Although both the Regulars and the Reserve forces wore the same grey and scarlet, the Regulars wore capes of solid scarlet while the Reserves wore grey capes trimmed with scarlet.

On duty we would wear a grey dress with two large front pockets and long sleeves that could be pushed back for ease of working. Our small shoulder capes edged with scarlet and a white headdress completed the working outfit. The Q.A. badge was always worn and today mine occupies a special space in the jewellery box on my bedroom dresser, a constant reminder of my war service.

Q.A./R. working uniforms. G. Aikens, second from right.

Outdoor winter uniform.

It seemed we were to have different outfits for different purposes or locations. For working in colder climates overseas pure woollen greatcoats, grey trimmed with scarlet, were worn. These were long, double-breasted affairs complete with a half-inch belt in the back and two pips, pieces of raised cloth indicating rank, on the shoulder. For special affairs and formal wear, we would be attired in the Q.A. Reserve officer dress uniform, still grey and scarlet, but made of a finer material than the everyday uniform. No headdress was worn.

On chilly days thick woollen cardigans were worn, and for going short distances outdoors, such as in and out of the hospital, we donned grey woollen cloaks lined with red. Even off duty, we were required to be in specific dress – a trim, grey tailor-made suit with white silk blouse and grey tie, and a regular-style grey army hat with brim. Except in emergencies, women were not permitted to wear trousers.

Once all medical testing, vaccinations and uniform-outfitting had been completed, we remained together at Tidworth to be educated for war. It was a charming spot close to other pleasant venues, and a few of us often walked into the nearby village of Amesbury for afternoon tea. The Nursing, or Sisters, Home at Tidworth had belonged to Lady Hamilton and was rumoured to have been a gift from Horatio Nelson. It was a lovely and gracious building set upon palatial grounds. Although the main interior of the building was cosy and warm, our quarters were cold, damp and musty and had us yearning for the day when we would be shipped off to our mobilization centres.

After being readied for active service, Q.A.s numbering in the hundreds together with doctors, orderlies, pharmacy and laboratory technicians, and army privates trained in first aid were assembled in one place to form a general hospital unit. This practice of gathering the unit and shipping it out together was known as mobilizing or making ready. This hospital unit would be sent to staff a general base hospital overseas.

Repackaging us into hospital staff units was difficult on friendships. Some friends with whom I had joined the army I didn't see again until much later. Some, I never saw again and I could only guess where their service might have taken them. No one ever knew where exactly their group would be sent, but we were soon to find out as we left Tidworth at the end of August for our mobilization centre.

Mobilization at Peebles Hydro, Scotland

After a long and tedious journey by train I arrived, one of a large group of people wanting only a pillow upon which to lay their weary heads, at our designated mobilization centre. Our exhaustion upon arrival at the centre was due in part, I suppose, to the fact that we were just recovering from the whole intricate process of entering the army, getting inoculations and suffering their effects, establishing new uniforms and all the other associated new army regimentation. It was a new type of discipline compared to that of civilian hospitals, and there was much to learn in a short time.

The centre for mobilization was a spot called Peebles near Edinburgh in Scotland. Peebles was a tiny town on the banks of the River Tweed, and it was known for the beautiful thick wools it produced. The town had been famous also for its healing waters, and we were housed in the Peebles Hydropathic, an elegant spa hotel which had previously enjoyed a reputation as a rather ritzy spot.

The structure was large and gracious and looked fairly modern – but the rooms were cold and furnished with only the bare necessities, one utter necessity being the tiny stone fireplace in each room. We gathered our own wood and the brisk mornings and cool evenings were cheerier and warmer as a result of crackling fires in those fireplaces.

Nurses kept arriving in Peebles from various parts of the country, but I saw no familiar faces, no one from my hospital in Sheffield. We all seemed to be strangers, thrown together like freshmen in a college dormitory.

We were informed, in our first lecture, that we would form the 95th General Base Hospital for overseas, although we weren't told just where overseas that was to be. We were lectured on secrecy and on how to deal with the men and other ranks of the military and, most importantly, the

The Peebles Hydropathic

war wounded, those people who were the very reason for our existence. Upon entering the Q.A.s as qualified State Registered Nurses, we were automatically commissioned as lieutenants.

Standing at attention the following day, I felt proud and patriotic and thought how extremely smart we all looked in our grey and scarlet Q.A. uniforms. Apart from having to look the part of army officers, we also had to act the part. To me, one of the strangest acts was saluting.

Once I was stopped in the street in Edinburgh by a senior officer. He had passed by and saluted; I had stood there thinking how very handsome and official he looked. He had come back to me and said rather abruptly, "When another officer or other rank salutes you, Sister, you don't just stand there and blush, you return the salute immediately." Well, we had lots of practice after that, especially on Princess Street, one of the main thoroughfares in Edinburgh. The whole city, it seemed, was in uniform, both British and Allied forces, and the colour and pageantry they added was a welcome sight to a city often cloaked in fog and drizzle.

No one could tell us for sure when we might depart for overseas, so we were given leave to visit friends and relatives. We bade tearful goodbyes and returned to Peebles.

It became embarrassing as we visited again and again, always thinking that this might be our last time before going overseas.

During one of my visits home, now to North Wales where my mother had temporarily located from Swansea, I realized what a very sad time it must be for my mother. My father had been about the same age as I when he left for France in 1916. He had been a conscientious objector, believing that war was senseless and an unnecessary waste of young life. Unfortunately, some members of the aristocracy thought otherwise and dubbed all such objectors as cowards. White feathers were sent to these individuals in the hope of humiliating them into joining up. My father hadn't wanted to receive one, so joined up.

Mother once showed me a thin plate of pressed metal about the size of a soldier's breast pocket, which my grandfather, who was in the sheet-metal business, had made for my father. It was meant to slip inside the breast pocket of his son's jacket in battle. It was rather pathetic, really. My grandfather obviously had no idea what sort of fighting was going on over there, but he had done his best to protect the heart of his son.

My father was killed in the Battle of the Somme, July 6, 1916, when I was just six months old. The metal plate was returned to my mother by the War Office in July 1916. It was accompanied by a photograph of my mother and me as a baby. If my mother harboured any fears about her only child going off to war, she kept them to herself.

Our mobilization at Peebles was enjoyable. We got to know each other and became accustomed to the routine which had been set down for us. We were awakened at 6:00 sharp each morning by the Royal Army Medical Corps (RAMC) drilling in front of our residence. As we had to be up and about anyway, we often dressed quickly to sit outside and watch the colourful array. There was something exciting about a smart army at drill.

Peebles group hiking the Moorfoot Hills. G. Aikens, centre

We attended numerous lectures during the day and sometimes were sent off to help with busy military hospitals in the surrounding area. In the off-duty hours a group of us would quite often hike through the Moorfoot Hills gathering blaeberries, similar to blueberries, or we would cycle into the nearby village of Galashiels, sometimes stopping for a picnic lunch along the way among the many old farms dotting the hillside. When time permitted, we would travel by bus into Edinburgh or Glasgow to explore the shops and attractions.

We always wore uniforms, always went with other officers, never with civilians, and always obeyed certain restrictions. Eyeing our uniforms, the townspeople would inquire when we'd be leaving for overseas and just where we would be posted. We had to shrug our shoulders and reply that we had no idea – which was the truth. We were waiting for orders to move and it could be a day, a week or a month until we received the word to go. In the meantime we kept occupied, checked in constantly and waited.

Our forays into the town centre had given us a chance to become better acquainted with the people of Peebles, and they seemed to have taken a liking to us. With Christmas a few weeks away, Peebles resembled a seasonal sketch of an old English village in winter with just the prescribed dusting of snow. We were invited to dances and social evenings and decided to put on a Christmas concert to show our appreciation and fondness for the townspeople.

There was no shortage of talent amongst us. The army assembled a decent-sounding band consisting of a sergeant, a few doctors and nurses, and a couple of other officers. A couple of the other Q.A.s, one of the sergeants and I composed a song about the people of Peebles and put it to the music of Elmer's Tune, a popular song at the time. We named our creation Peebles Air and rehearsed diligently.

With all of us working on different skits, songs and dances we knew we would have a worthwhile production. We had chosen a date and time, put up a few posters and made tickets to hand out at the door. It must have come as quite a shock to the people of Peebles when, a few days before the scheduled Christmas concert, the whole general hospital vanished without a trace.

At Sea

We had been awakened at 2:00 a.m. with orders to be ready to move in precisely one hour. We were well aware that the British Army waited for no stragglers; one hour later found us settled on the train, Peebles a fond memory. We departed stealthily from the station in Peebles to destinations unknown to us. Because we couldn't see out of the train's blacked-out windows, we had no idea where we were going, and could only guess, listening for the smallest familiar sounds. The lot of us filled our little train to capacity. After what seemed like a long, tiresome journey, we arrived at a seaport. Those from Scotland amongst the crowd thought it might be a place known as Greenock.

A damp and misty December dawn greeted us as we quietly detrained and got onto tenders, those long, flat boats used to transfer large numbers of people from dockside to ocean liners waiting offshore and used mainly for reasons of secrecy. The process was exhilarating and at the same time a little frightening and lonely. I hugged my arms tightly around me, shivering in the chill wind, wondering why on earth I had put myself into this situation. The whisper of a briny wind off the sea was the only sound.

The Q.A.s were huddled close on the tenders and surrounded by handsome young men. Although we may have been a bit scared, I believe we all felt very safe. I wonder now if those men had felt safe too, surrounded by all of us nurses. It probably was the last thing in the world they would have been thinking about.

Things were happening quickly now. Orders came for us to prepare to move off and the tenders began to groan and shift underfoot, steering towards something hidden in the fog. After what seemed like ages we found ourselves alongside the mighty grey hull of a huge ship. I had seen many huge ships in the Swansea docks but never from below, and the massive hull looked foreboding.

I could see no name printed on the hull but had heard someone say this ship might be the SS Strathallan. While waiting to go on board, I thought about my father crossing to France with the Royal Welsh Fusiliers. I wondered what sort of ship he had been on, what his thoughts were had been. Was he scared? Would he have been proud to see his only child, his daughter, heading off to serve her country as he had?

Convoy

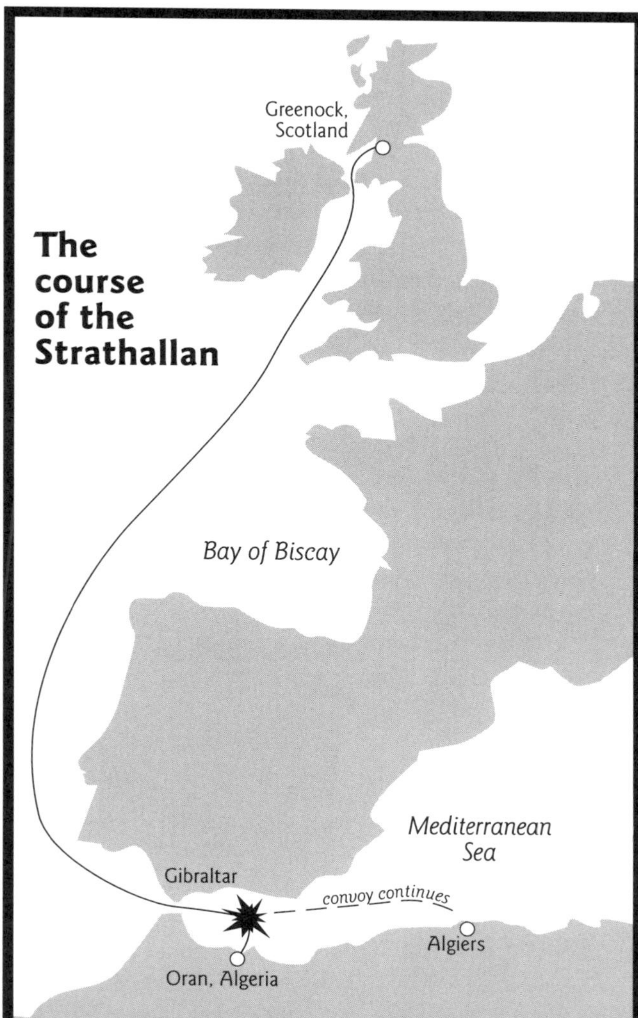
The course of the Strathallan
Greenock, Scotland
Bay of Biscay
Mediterranean Sea
Gibraltar
convoy continues
Algiers
Oran, Algeria

The SS Strathallan

How I got aboard the ship I am not sure, as it happened so quickly, a blur of orders and uniforms passing by in haste and then there we all were. Once on deck, our cabins were assigned immediately. There were three or four people to a cabin, all crammed into an incredibly tiny box which contained bunk beds and just enough space left for a person to turn around in without bumping her cabinmates if she were very careful!

Our belongings for overseas had been painstakingly packed into regulation small black steel trunks. They had been kept always weighed and ready to travel. Anything we took out of the trunk could be replaced by its equal, and the trunk and its contents could be inspected at any time without notice. These black trunks containing our precious belongings had been jammed into the ship's hold, and we had only our small kit bags to keep us supplied with clothing and toiletries until we landed.

Cabins assigned, we were at liberty to wander around. Despite the early hour, we were advised to walk around the ship and get acquainted with every nook and cranny. This experience resembled a walking tour of a large four-storey hotel. All the little spaces which had been fashionable shops full of cruise ship clothing and souvenirs had been vacated and put to use for equipment storage and other such purposes.

Having been up since 2:00 that morning with precious little to eat, and after ambling around breathing the salt sea air, we were thankful to hear the call for breakfast around 5:30 a.m.

Later that morning, as I lay on my bunk reading, I heard the ship's siren signal the first of many lifeboat drills. We were to become well acquainted with our lifeboat stations and be able to reach them rapidly from wherever we

The SS Strathallan in pre-war peacetime service

happened to be on the ship with, of course, the mandatory lifejackets in place over our skirted uniforms. As ridiculous as it seemed for this lifestyle, women were still not permitted to wear trousers!

This ship which served as our home for approximately the next two weeks was a Peninsular and Oriental Steam Navigation Company liner, or a P&O, as it was sometimes called, and it was indeed the SS Strathallan. In peacetime it had served as a luxury liner, cruising with vacationers on a UK/Bombay/Australia circuit. Just before war was declared in 1939 the Strathallan had been running from Australia to the Fiji Islands. But in times of emergency and in war, liners like this one were commandeered by the British Government, converted for war purposes and crewed by the Royal Navy.

The first breakfast had been welcome, as we were starving. A piece of dry bread would have tasted excellent. But we must have looked somewhat incredulously at the ensuing three-course meals placed before us. Having just come from war-rationed Great Britain, we hadn't seen such variety and quantity of food for a very long time. In Britain we might have had one egg and one ounce of butter and very little meat, perhaps four ounces, to last us for a week. Here our menu included succulent steak and fish dishes, mouthwatering desserts, thick, crusty breads and more. This was fine while we were stationary, but after the ship had left port and was travelling up to speed, I would find that I could not stomach very much of anything except perhaps a dry roll.

The dining room was elegant, but sometimes for a change of scenery we would take a sandwich or a piece of fruit to one of the ship's lounges. Apart from serving as places to sit and read while munching on a snack, the lounges provided a quiet refuge in which to write letters or simply to become better acquainted with our shipmates.

Under Way to the War Zone – December 1942

The Strathallan remained at anchor for three very long days. Finally, after much speculation and anticipation, it slipped out to sea sometime during the night of the third day, probably around December 10. At the sound of the ship's engines and the now obvious lulling motion of the sea beneath us, we knew the waiting was over. My cabinmates and I dashed at once to the portholes; what we thought we might see I'm not sure – it was simply a reflex action to look outside. There was nothing except the same damp, grey mist that had welcomed us on board and had stayed with us while we sat.

It was a strange feeling, leaving my country and going to a war zone, and, stranger and more frightening still, not knowing where that war zone was. The troops we had met back in Peebles used to joke about the peculiarities of war, and I recall one of them saying to me, "If you had been equipped with white helmets and summer uniforms, Sister, you can be sure they'd land you in the Arctic. If on the other hand you had been given fur coats and woollies, you'd be sure to wind up in the tropics." This wasn't a comment on the vagaries of fitting-out, but on the lengths our command would go to for secrecy. I couldn't remember what was in my trunk, although I had packed and repacked it many times.

Only the War Office knew our destination, but whoever left the docks that night would be with us in the hospital which we would set up. At least the lot of us from the Hydro in Peebles would still be together, so the friendships formed at the Hydro would see us through difficult times ahead. One of my friends, Nora Wells, had not returned after her last leave from Peebles and I didn't know why. I was sorry about that. We did meet again some years later.

No one slept. We were too curious and talkative. We knew there would be no turning back now and we kept dashing back and forth to the portholes, peering out. We thought we could discern other ships far off in the distance, surreal and ghostly, looming up through the fog. And everywhere around us was completely still.

I had some difficulty adjusting to the new bunk and the rocking motion of the boat and tried to ignore the everpresent seasickness. It helped to get out on deck and take some deep breaths. Our main exercise was to walk around the deck, and my roommates and I, along with many others aboard, were always up early to do just that.

Our hospital group from Peebles was not the only group on board, and we soon got to know some of the others from different mobilization centres who were sailing with us. Together we comprised a little over 4000 troops, mostly British, plus 250 Q.A.s, 431 crew, 35 passengers and 296 military officers. The latter included some high-ranking U.S. and Allied officers and possibly some U.S. and Allied intelligence officers.

It was rumoured that one of the ship's officers was a relative of King George VI and that Margaret Bourke-White, the war photographer for the American magazine Life, was on board. We were certain we would see nothing of them!

The next afternoon another Sister and I walked the deck once again. We stopped at one point to look down upon a gaping hole, which had previously served as a swimming pool for the ship's peacetime guests, and which was now covered by long wooden planks, serving as a sort of stage. The troops often assembled on that makeshift stage to sing and entertain the rest of us with their remarkable wit and eclectic talents.

We spied a couple arm in arm on the stage and thought she looked rather like Margaret Bourke-White. Even in wartime there were shipboard romances, it seems. We saw a lot of Bourke-White, and she was usually in the company of a tall, handsome officer. She was an attractive, dynamic and truly delightful lady who seemed surrounded by a neverending energy and glow.

She led quite a bit of the singing and accompanied the troops on her accordion, such were her multiple talents! She circulated amongst us all, fitting in like one of the boys, and was quite popular. There was one song that the men made her sing over and over with all its numerous verses – Frankie and Johnny Were Sweethearts, and Bourke-White had just the right American accent for it. She was a good morale-booster, helping the troops forget for the moment where they were headed.

By our third day at sea, the skies above had turned black and turbulent, although the seas remained relatively calm. I would have much preferred to sit on deck in the fresh air, but we were advised to stay below, as an oncoming storm was gaining in force and intensity. We were apparently approaching the Bay of Biscay now.

Our ship was travelling in convoy; or so we were told – we hardly saw any other ships. This invisible convoy of ours, known as the escorting convoy KMFS, consisted of ships carrying troops, provisions and equipment to the war zone. Although the Strathallan was not a battleship, there were a few guns on deck for use in case of attack.

The convoy travelled in single file, surrounded on all sides by armed escort ships together with an aircraft carrier. We could just make out the aircraft carrier as it bobbed up and down way ahead of us. It gave us a sense of security, but it was probably quite a target. We heard that if one ship got hit the rest must keep going; no stopping to pick anyone up unless ordered to. What a horrible thought for both the disabled ship and the helpless onlookers!

Between lifeboat drills, usually about three or four per day, and other routine shipboard army manoeuvres there was some spare time which I used wisely to catch up on reading or to learn new skills. One new skill was the game of bridge, which I agreed to learn one evening in the ship's lounge. It was far more difficult than whist, which I had been used to playing at home, but at least the mental aerobics served to take my mind off the war for a time. While seated in my foursome that evening, one of the girls, who always seemed to get the news before anyone else, said that a German submarine had been spotted and was keeping a close watch on us.

We had been constantly warned that we must do nothing to alert the enemy to our whereabouts, not even throw a bit of orange peel overboard, because the German submarines were always waiting and watching for the slightest sign of unsuspecting British ships. With so many ships in the water it was perhaps a little unrealistic to think we could sneak through the seas by holding on to our orange peel. We didn't think the German subs would risk surfacing amongst all the British ships, and we figured they were probably not keen on attacking a convoy unless one ship happened to stray off course.

Storm-tossed

From the way the cards kept sliding across the table and the difficulty of staying upright in my chair, I knew that Mother Nature was preparing to unleash her fury. I ventured over to a porthole and through the raindrops and misted glass watched as what looked like ten-foot waves foamed and churned, smashing angrily against the sides of the ship. The bridge game didn't go too much longer; the singsong we had planned to hold around the piano later that evening was postponed. Most of us returned to our cabins to wait out the storm. There was no dinner for me and no sleep. It seemed that the sea was trying its best to shake up the ship and throw us all out of our cabins. I was glad I had company because I was scared.

One of my cabinmates tried to put on her pyjamas. It looked funny as she tried to stand on one foot and poke the other through a pyjama leg while the floor pitched this way and that, but not for long. She wound up in the ship's hospital with a fractured leg.

That put a stop to anyone in our cabin wearing pyjamas and we made alternate arrangements! On the heels of that incident, likely on account of the foul weather, we were finally permitted to wear slacks, and we wore them day and night until reaching our destination. We agreed, it simply had become too dangerous to change in and out of them!

By dawn's first light the seas had subsided only slightly, but we were able to get up on deck for a very short period of fresh air. The tables, chairs and sofas in the dining room had been chained down and the main lounge was off limits to us. The large mahogany upright piano which we had planned to sing around had evidently been gleefully careening into the other furniture in the night and was now chained in a far corner like an errant puppy.

Other casualties than our roommate now graced the beds of the tiny hospital ward set up below. A friend and I decided to visit our cabinmate. The small hospital on the lower deck carried passengers who were sick or had suffered accidents during the voyage out – like our cabinmate – and who were not considered war wounded.

On the way down to the hospital we passed the hold where most of the troops were housed. Such a dark, cramped space for those men, especially for the duration of a journey that wasn't a pleasant one anyway, but I suppose it was the only way to convey over 4000 troops.

Our companion was reclining comfortably. She would now have to turn around and go back to the U.K. when we reached our port of call, and she was naturally upset and annoyed that she would be going home as the result of a silly accident.

The storm didn't want to go away. Rain squalls were frequent and winds escalated back to gale force. We couldn't see any of the ships in our convoy; they seemed to have scattered. Indeed, we later learned that two of the boats experiencing difficulty with the rough seas had strayed off course and were missing.

Amid persistent rumours about the enemy submarine, our commanding officer put us through our lifeboat drill yet again. These drills never lasted very long, and I imagine the routine we went through was the same as it was on all ocean liners, but more frequent. There might have been more people allotted to each boat in wartime. We were told that there were 80 people to each lifeboat. The edges of the deck were lined with wooden lifeboats. In addition, there were rows of stacked rafts which could hold 20–30 people each. We all knew that there was insufficient lifesaving equipment for everyone on board, but I suppose in wartime chances were taken and one had to make do with what was available.

Initially, drill times had been posted on the bulletin boards, and we would appear en masse at our lifeboat stations as the ship's alarm screeched on schedule. We were instructed in the technique of donning lifejackets quickly and shedding them just as fast. Little funny-looking tin helmets completed our outfits. In the beginning we went through this routine at least once a day. After a while we could expect the alarms to come by surprise any time during the night or while raising a forkful of dinner to our mouths. Those lifebelts and tin helmets seemed to form a second skin, as we decked out in them so often.

Day seven at sea, or perhaps it was day ten? I was losing track. Gradually the ocean swells subsided. The cook prepared quite a feast, and I was able to enjoy the roast beef and Yorkshire pudding preceded by appetizers of a sort and followed by sweets. Quite an accomplishment for one who, even as a child, had never been a good sailor. Being on this ship evoked all sorts of memories of sailing on short day-trips from my home in Swansea, South Wales, to the seaside resort of Ilfracombe just across the Bristol Channel. This trip, though, was quite a revelation. Proud of myself for not feeling the least bit queasy, I retired to the ship's lounge after dinner and played a few hands of bridge. I had improved considerably and was enjoying the game itself and the camaraderie and cheerfulness.

Landfall

"I think it's Gibraltar," I heard someone shout as I was awakened late in the night by voices. I quickly threw off the covers, and not bothering with slippers, tiptoed barefoot to the porthole, where I came face to face with a massive pinkish rock – the Rock of Gibraltar. I wondered if we would land here. Our ship was stopped, but we didn't know why. After my roommates and I had discussed all sorts of possible theories, we went back to bed, talking until the last of us drifted off to sleep.

By dawn's first light, the great rock was behind us, and we were left comparing our descriptions of the sighting. One or two of the destroyers in our convoy had apparently stopped over in Gibraltar to refuel and land passengers and stores. We also learned that the two boats that had strayed off course in the storm had arrived safely in Gibraltar. A few of our escort ships had turned back for the U.K. at Gibraltar.

The disturbing bit of information was that one of the lead boats had, the previous evening, received a sounding off its port side. No chances had been taken and a full pattern was fired although nothing was hit. Rumour had it that officers in charge believed that fish had set off the sounding devices, although as a further precaution the course out from Gibraltar had been altered.

The Mediterranean waters were calm, and I went for a long walk around the deck. After a good twenty minutes or so, I was once again hungry and was quite looking forward to breakfast. Having conquered last evening's roast beef, I was more than prepared to tackle the plate of bacon and eggs which was soon before me. To think of all those bacon-and-egg breakfasts I had been missing!

The aircraft carrier which had been escorting us was no longer in sight, and I missed being able to see it, but I felt quite safe and that seemed to be the general feeling around me.

Although without a calendar, I knew that Christmas Eve must be close. It seemed funny to think of Christmas in a ship on its way to war. Now, along with our usual songs like "You Are My Sunshine," "Roll Out the Barrel" and "The Quartermaster Store," we sang seasonal songs such as "White Christmas," the Bing Crosby song which was to become very popular. Many of the troops had produced mouth organs, which made everything sound festive.

I had heard so often how beautiful the Mediterranean was. In the evenings, the sea was like black ink, a perfect canvas to reflect the millions of stars shimmering overhead. This particular evening was one of the most lovely, calm and warm with just the slightest hint of a breeze gently blowing tiny wisps of my hair across my face.

We were scheduled to arrive at our destination in a day or so, and I had placed my belongings in my kit bag, leaving out just a few necessities for the night. Most of the others on board were also preparing to disembark, eager to be held captive no longer. We were all late going to bed that night; perhaps the evening was just too beautiful to miss. Eventually, one by one, we made our way to our cabins, but I doubt if any of us slept soundly, as our thoughts were refocussing on what lay ahead. We knew by all the rumours circulating that we would not be going to Europe or the Far East.

It was well past midnight when I slipped between the cosy flannel sheets of my bunk and went right off to sleep. I was in a very hot country, perhaps India, riding on the back of an elephant, of all things. The huge animal was swaying from side to side, rocking me in the saddle so that I had to grip the reins very tightly. His feet on the ground made a groaning sound, monotonous and hypnotizing. The elephant was moving ahead more quickly now and I was frightened, holding on for dear life. I tried to warn him of the huge ravine in front of him, but he couldn't see it and then it was too late. Suddenly he was down and I lost hold of the reins and fell with him, hitting the ground hard.

Torpedoed – December 21, 1942

"My God, we've been hit!" A terrific explosion, then a paralysing silence. If the alarm bells sounded, I don't remember hearing them. But I do remember the speed with which my cabinmates and I tugged on sweaters and boots, thrust arms through greatcoats, pulled lifejackets over our heads, tying up both sides with hands that seemed to have four thumbs and, panic-stricken, dashed out the cabin door. We couldn't hear the familiar low humming of the ship's engine, usually faintly conspicuous in the background. The sounds of voices came to us as others on board were roused – exclamations of disbelief, shouts for order and haste.

Lifeboat drill had paid off; so far, the whole procedure was now simply falling into place. I'm sure I could have done it in my sleep and as it was, at almost 2:30 in the morning and with the shock of what had just occurred, I was in a bit of a daze.

Unfortunately, the drills simply couldn't have prepared us for many of the things that we were to encounter that night. Our drills had prepared us to mobilize from any location, so the drills had interrupted us at every conceivable waking activity. But this time almost all the ship's occupants had been asleep or at the very least in their quarters, all below deck, the therefore over 4000 of us were thronging the routes to the deck.

Drill conditions had included daylight or artificial light. This time, in the black of the early morning, there was no semblance of light. All power was off. I was just one of a huge apprehensive exodus shuffling along the dark corridors.

In drill the ship, though always rocking to some degree, had been upright. Now she was listing heavily to port. Climbing the stairways was like scaling the side of a mountain. We looked for our stations. There were no lights, blackness engulfed us. "There had been no alarm sounded," someone shouted.

One or two of the wooden cabin doors along the ship's darkened passageways refused to open despite all efforts to push on them as we passed by on our way to the deck above. We were helpless, caught between the sorrowful pleas, the banging of hands from the other side of the door, and the knowledge that if we didn't get up to the deck as soon as possible we would be facing a certain death. There was no time to think about the pitiful dilemma facing us; we had to get out fast.

As we passed empty cabins, doors ajar, I was shocked to see some of my fellow passengers quietly walk into a room and snatch up belongings which another passenger had left behind in his hurry to get above deck. I couldn't believe that at a time of disaster like this, people could think of anything else but getting off a sinking ship. It was the first time I had even heard the word "looting" or knew what it meant. I was shocked and disappointed.

We had just about reached the outside and I could smell the familiar salt spray mingled with a burning smell – or was it my overactive imagination? From behind me someone called for volunteer nurses to go down with the patients in the ship's hospital. They couldn't be moved, they were too sick, there wasn't time, there wasn't room enough on the lifeboats and smaller rafts.

"Go down?" I thought. The ship was actually going down – this was no dream. How could I run away and leave those people helpless, probably to die slowly without any chance of survival? How would they go? Just sink below the water as it quickly flooded the floors, rising higher and higher swallowing everything in sight?

I just couldn't go back. I felt so guilty and knew that there were others behind me who would go back to the hospital to hold hands and weep with the patients. I wished that I hadn't heard that call, but I hoped that God above would forgive me and understand my strong desire to go on with my life. I wasn't ready to die, not yet. If that happened in battle, so be it, I had resigned myself to that possibility. But not now, not yet. I kept moving on, finally ascending the last step. I was on deck at last.

On deck, hundreds of voices mingled, high and low, shouting, talking, crying and questioning, louder and louder. A shot rang out and the voices subsided. We were told later that some of the troops who had heard that there were not enough lifeboats and rafts wanted to jump overboard. An officer had fired a shot to stop any panic. But panic was minimal and confusion prevalent.

We had been on deck about an hour when a second explosion rocked the ship. We watched as two white rockets were fired – a distress signal to the rest of the convoy.

Now that we were facing abandonment of the ship, we had to actually get the lifeboats assembled, board the boats and then lower the fully loaded vessels to the sea below. "Where did we all go, who got assigned to what boat, who was to go and who could not?" I silently asked myself. I think I must have been panicking, because of course we had gone through this whole routine before and there were competent people in charge who knew exactly what to do. We knew from lifeboat drill which boat to go to; I had been assigned to boat number 12.

As we assembled we heard the most ghastly screams and splashing. I couldn't see a thing but I found out later that a couple of the boats had capsized as they were being lowered and the occupants had been thrown into the water. It was horrible. I heard those screams for weeks afterward.

We assumed that the German submarine which we thought had left us had in fact been tailing us all the way and finally seized its chance to torpedo us. Or perhaps we had been hit by another sub lying in wait for us on the other side of Gibraltar – the supposed fish that had triggered the alarm signal. Anything was possible. Why had we thought just yesterday that we were safe?

After making the painful decision to get myself saved instead of going down with the ship, I climbed over the railing into my lifeboat. I and probably 60–100 others, more than permitted, jammed into the boat, which was then precariously and slowly but safely lowered to the churning waters below.

The hit had flooded our lifeboats with water. In our boat the water came up to my knees. As we were lowered, another boat was being lowered above us and the water from that one splashed over us. It really seemed as if I was in someone else's nightmare.

"Am I really floating here in the middle of the Mediterranean in a small wooden boat watching our beautifully huge and, until now safe, ship go down?" I wondered. I had no capacity to be scared; the whole predicament was so unreal.

At the Mercy of the Sea

"If you don't all help to row this boat, we'll be going down with the ship." That booming voice out of nowhere belonged to one of our matrons. Our lifeboat, filled to capacity and sitting low in the water, was within a few feet of the huge hulk of a ship which all of a sudden looked more menacing than friendly.

The Strathallan's Indian crew who had been assigned to be oarsmen were sitting motionless in stunned silence, just as awestruck and gripped with fear as the rest of us. Therefore, we all had to be strong together. We couldn't at this point afford to rely on anyone else. Someone started singing "Row, row, row your boat" and one by one we joined in both singing and rowing until our arms and lungs both were aching.

And then our matron again, focussing my drifting thoughts. "We're drifting back towards the ship. You've got to pick up those oars and row, now. If you can't find oars, for heavens sakes use your arms, we've got to get away from that ship or we'll be sucked under with it." And I suddenly realized that Matron was right. When an ocean liner like the Strathallan goes down, it creates a huge whirlpool of suction and pulls everything nearby down with it. We rowed like mad then, and before long, we had managed to row our boat to safer waters.

Not that far away from us still, the Strathallan was silhouetted against the faint light of dawn. This huge, floating home, where we had sparked friendships, listened to and ruminated over various suppositions, marvelled over sumptuous meals and then again wondered if we could ever look at food again, this vessel that had carried us proudly from our country, was now being abandoned. It seemed impossible that yesterday I was enjoying an elegant meal in the ship's dining room, which was now undoubtedly swamped beneath the murky waters of the ocean. I felt a deep sense of loss and a sadness for that magnificent object which was now sinking. I wondered if everyone who could be had been taken off safely. I heard that many of the troops had remained on board for the moment, and so probably had managed to get everyone else off. I hoped so.

To my surprise, Margaret Bourke-White was in our lifeboat. She was seated at the other end with two nurses flanking her and an officer. She didn't look very upset even though her usual officer friend wasn't nearby. As a matter of fact, she had managed to save some of her photographic equipment and was now busy taking snaps in all directions. Bourke-White's account and photos of the torpedoing eventually appeared, somewhat embellished (as though embellishment was needed!) in Life Magazine.

Conditions in our little boat were frightful. Although the weather was fairly calm, the Royal Navy was dropping depth charges, and the waters exploded and foamed like mini-volcanoes, wetting us constantly with frothy ocean spray. We had to bail constantly, using our tin helmets to scoop up the water. We assumed the navy was still trying to sink the submarine that had torpedoed the Strathallan.

I had a tiny silver flask of brandy in my satchel, a gift I had received from someone while on leave from Peebles. I offered it to the injured in our boat and never got the flask back. I missed it for its sentimental value, but I hoped it had done one of those injured survivors some good and maybe helped to save a life.

There was more light now, and as I surveyed the clusters of boats bobbing up and down in the sea I felt comforted knowing that I wasn't alone. Just then, someone shouted out and pointed over the water at the ominous black periscope of a submarine. We saw an oil slick on the water and more depth charges were heard and felt by everyone. Again, we were tossed about like a ball on a racquet, but we stayed afloat, albeit low in the water.

We could see quite plainly the two destroyers ploughing the seas all around us but neither of them stopping. I could still make out the Strathallan and a destroyer close by her. Somebody was shouting through a megaphone. We must have watched the boats for at least two hours, or so it seemed, and then we were looking at only the sea. In silence. The occasional sound of survivors pulling their coats more tightly around them, or muted conversation at one end of the boat. A slapping of water on the wood of the boat with an occasional larger wave. Some noise from neighbouring lifeboats. But nothing else.

I felt how cool the air was; with only my greatcoat, saturated with water, to cover me and feet that were soaking wet, I was shivering violently and quite nauseous, not only because of the rocking of the boat, but with the thought that perhaps we would be left to perish out here, just not important enough in the overall scheme of things. I remembered I couldn't swim. "But then where would I swim to?" I thought. I must have giggled then, for someone nudged me from behind. A plane, looking like a bird who had lost its flock, circled overhead and was gone. Someone said we had been in the lifeboat for twelve hours.

All the oars we had used in our frantic attempt to escape the suction of the large ship had long since been lost overboard. Most of our little tin helmets had also disappeared, probably while bailing the boat. Someone had said something earlier about tossing the helmets overboard but this wasn't a popular idea as many were using their helmets as seasick containers. Most of us still had our survivors' rations; mine were untouched in a little tin. I had no appetite. I dug my hands into the deep pockets of my greatcoat and stamped my feet together, hoping to generate a bit of warmth, and I let my eyelids close for a moment, to hope and to pray.

And then it was over. From nowhere a miraculous sight was speeding towards our little boat. But perhaps I was delirious and this was a mirage? Possibly, I mused, as I watched the huge destroyer slow its pace and silently, smoothly, nose its way in until it could safely move toward us no further.

Voices were shouting instructions and warnings from above and then instructions came from Matron again to use whatever we could to propel our boat alongside the destroyer. No, this was no dream. This destroyer was part of the Royal Navy and one of the two that had stayed behind the convoy to help. I squinted up at the bow and read the name "Verity," a name which I will never forget.

A sharp slapping sound alerted me to watch the next procedure before becoming a part of it. A rope ladder was dropped from way up above. It looked simple to climb, especially as I was anxious to leave the damp confines of the cramped lifeboat. However, to get onto the ladder from the lifeboat and then actually to climb the thing proved difficult. I wanted to get on board that destroyer as fast as possible, but in my seasick state my feet simply refused to grip the rungs of the ladder.

After more than a few frustrating and embarrassing attempts I finally managed to do it. The thought of warm clothing and a safe ship must have coaxed my feet onward, and it is possible I had some help from behind me, for I was at last on board. People were lifted from the boats below, some luckily just suffering from sprains or minor fractures, others not so fortunate, soldiers and Sisters dead from shock or exposure. One fellow alone on a raft, pushing with only his hands, pulled up to the boat yelling out, "Hey taxi!" We thought he should receive a medal just for his marvellous attitude.

The rumours we had heard were confirmed aboard the destroyer. Our ship had been pursued for three days by a pack of submarines. We also learned that the stormy weather had been the most savage and relentless storm that the ship's captain had experienced in 45 years at sea, with waves sometimes 60 feet high. Probably all boats of the convoy had been targeted, but ours was the only one hit. We were told the Strathallan had been struck by two torpedoes and the one that had hit the engine room had killed two engineers and two crew. We also heard that two other crewmembers and a small number of passengers and nursing Sisters were also lost.

Although they were supposed to continue with the rest of the convoy, the commanding officers of the two destroyers had felt that there was a good chance of sinking the attacking submarine and then safely taking on survivors. The destroyers had spotted us before going after the sub, but the submarine got top billing. Only after dropping the depth charges and sinking the submarine had the Verity turned around to rescue us. Those men running the destroyer knew we sure as heck weren't going anywhere in the meantime. The HMS Verity picked up 1200 of the survivors, an effort which was officially commended by the British navy shortly after the rescue.

Our flotilla of lifeboats and myriad rafts were left to fend for themselves in the oily waters below. The sea had been covered with oil slicks from disabled submarines and other ships, and as we had been constantly splashed with the greasy water, our hair and clothing were coated in oil. The exceedingly handsome crew of the destroyer only seemed thrilled to see this tangled, oily group of survivors in their midst. Stories abounded on the ship, and despite our weariness, we talked and listened for hours.

It's not possible to describe accurately the sheer joy of being rescued after accepting earlier that this was probably the end. Above and beyond the happiness of the rescue was the post-rescue. This saw the lot of us, oil-soaked and giddy, standing around the sides of the ship with jubilant smiles on our faces, mugs of hot Ovaltine in hand. I felt very safe and completely in love with the whole Royal Navy. A quick wash, warm clothing and a boat that wasn't rocking from side to side, and realized that I was hungry. The word seasickness lost its meaning as we devoured Spam sandwiches with more steaming mugs of tea and Ovaltine, feeling wonderful.

In the distance the Strathallan listed helplessly. The only sadness, apart from the loss of life, was the loss of our ship. We could see heavy clouds of smoke and flame coming from her funnel. We got under way shortly and left her behind, but we were updated along the route as to her fate.

The fire that had started in the engine room raged for over an hour and was finally completely out of control. The rescue tugs didn't get to the scene as fast as had been expected and all remaining crew were ordered to abandon ship. The boat that was towing her had turned her loose.

Almost an hour later, another boat resumed the job, pulling the disabled Strathallan towards Oran, Algeria. More crew went aboard to try to save the ship, but three hours later it was a losing battle. Just after 4:00 p.m. on December 22 the Strathallan sank 12 miles outside of Oran.

North Africa

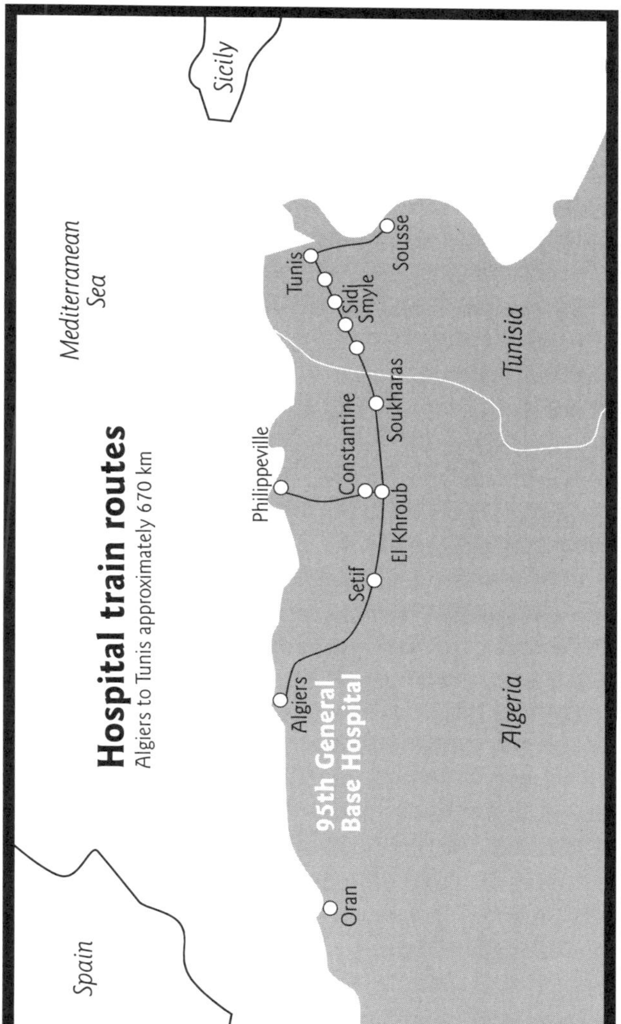

Onward to North Africa

Where the Strathallan had left off on its plotted course, the Verity now picked up, and we continued on an altered route to North Africa, although we hadn't previously known for sure that North Africa was our destination. Our rescue still seemed a trifle unreal to me, like something I would see in a movie.

The sun shone like silver from behind the frosty blue skies onto the calm waters below, and the sea was transformed into a sheet of blue satin, magical yet serene. The remainder of the journey was peaceful, and most of us spent the time sleeping. The destroyer quickly transported its newly acquired passengers to Oran, a seaport between Gibraltar and Algiers, and then it was goodbye to the ship and crew who had given us a chance to continue our lives.

Our destroyer was one of many ships picking up survivors and dropping them ashore so they could be driven to their eventual destinations. Large buses were waiting at dockside to take survivors into Algiers; no sooner had we disembarked than we were queuing to board the bus.

And none of us with any more possessions than what we were wearing. I had my greatcoat, sweater, slacks, shoes, lifejacket, one glove and a red suede satchel holding survivor's rations and a couple of other little things. The rest of our belongings had gone down with the Strathallan in those small black trunks which we had so painstakingly weighed, measured, packed and repacked ages ago in Peebles. But we were alive and well. And we were ready to get on with the work ahead of us.

At the last minute there was a change in plans. Those in charge decided we would stay the night on another troopship called the Duchess of Richmond. Sleep was next to impossible as, through the night and into the wee hours of the morning, the air was filled with the sounds of ships continuing to arrive with survivors from the Strathallan and perhaps from other ships that had suffered the same fate.

There was a neverending reunion of friends and shipmates. We hadn't been together on the Strathallan long enough to have made intimate friendships, but I was happy to meet up with those from Peebles whom I had known longer. All except for two Q.A.s whom I kept inquiring about. Someone told me that one of them had been in one of the capsized boats. The other Q.A. I didn't see or hear about for over three years.

There were quite a few survivors coming off the ships on stretchers and being lifted into waiting ambulances. I didn't recognize anyone. I met two of the R.A. officers I had played bridge with. One of them, unable to get on a lifeboat or raft, had found something to serve as a makeshift raft and had clung to that for hours before being rescued.

The stories continued. We heard that two of the group from Peebles, people in the boat which had been overturned, swam with a nonswimmer, a red-haired girl, trying desperately to reach a lifeboat or raft. They had become exhausted and couldn't hang on to her any longer. Wanting to save her yet knowing that the three of them might drown, they had let her go and kept going on their own. It was an awful decision. They never knew who she was. We never really knew what became of anyone as there was so much secrecy. Rumours were rampant, and they were all we could go by.

Someone else again related the account of the Royal Navy destroyers bombing the hell out of the submarines chasing us. I wondered why I felt so happy, all those men blown to pieces. But this was war, wasn't it? We weren't hearing it on radio or wireless or watching Pathe Gazette. We were right in the middle of it. Some of our friends might have already given their lives for their country and we hadn't even started our nursing service yet. They would never complete the noble work they had set out to do.

Orders came early the next morning to board the buses which were still patiently waiting. We transferred after a while to trains and finally switched to army transport convoy. It was a long, tiring journey, being bumped about on the uneven roads past sparse scenery.

At practically every railway station we spotted Arab children selling oranges. Once or twice we stopped and bought some of their fruit and they would smile and nod and wave us on.

Algiers – December 1942

We were a dishevelled, dust-covered bunch when we finally set foot in Algiers a day or two before Christmas. We couldn't see very much of the city, as it was thoroughly blacked out, and anyway our only thoughts were of getting some sleep.

But not yet. About an hour after arriving in Algiers and waiting for what we supposed were further orders, we were informed we were to be transported to a small encampment on the outskirts of the city. We would set up a base hospital there and would be billeted temporarily in an old orphanage. So it was back in the trucks and on the road again. We were met with a small air raid, but we were too physically drained to care. Upon our eventual arrival at the suburb of Ben Aknoun, we went through the now familiar routine and were then settled into our rooms at the orphanage. It took only a minute or two to fall asleep.

The next morning my roommates and I were a sight to behold as we tried to cope with wash basins and lavatories which stood only a foot off the ground. But in an orphanage, what could one expect?

We stepped outside, curious, and found that our orphanage accommodation was settled in the midst of a citrus grove! Adjacent to the orphanage sat a huge French museum which had been taken over by the British and converted into a general hospital. The grounds of the orphanage and the museum were cluttered with patrolling armed guards. French gendarmes stationed there temporarily mingled with the British guards, although the French were later replaced with a contingent of British sentries.

In wartime, the base hospitals were set up in strategically safe locations, but they also had to be easily accessible. For the most part this meant they were found in seaport towns or cities where they could receive the wounded soldiers and dispatch some homeward for further convalescence.

Our central duty as Q.A.s was to tend to the war wounded, and if this also meant following the men in battle, we did. A wounded soldier was immediately taken by stretcher to a casualty clearance station. From there he would be taken to an ambulance, or hospital, train. We worked aboard the ambulance trains, administering medical care to wounded soldiers as they were being transported to the base hospital. These trains were travelling hospital units fully equipped with medical staff that crisscrossed the country following the progress of the British forces.

After transfer from train to the more stabilized hospitals nearby, medical treatment and nursing care would continue. The seriously wounded would eventually be transferred to a hospital ship destined for the U.K. to receive further medical attention.

Not all soldiers went home. Those who weren't as badly injured were cared for and then sent back to the front for active duty.

Any building capable of holding at least a thousand people, such as the museum next to our orphanage, would be expropriated for hospital purposes. A field hospital would have already arrived along with the first attacking forces and our convoy was bringing in the necessities such as hospital equipment, bed clothing, extra uniforms for the men, pharmacy and laboratory equipment and

Nurses in battledress, G. Aikens at right

stretchers. Unfortunately, that convoy didn't bring in uniforms for the women, only for the men.

When we got off the boat in Oran we had nothing; no uniforms, not even any underwear! Our equipment had arrived in Algiers before us, but replacement uniforms had not yet arrived and we were therefore issued with men's battledress – khaki shirts and trousers, wide black leather belts, black army boots and socks, and even men's underwear! Fit was approximate. Because of lack of experience and too many buttons (no zippers in this war, unfortunately), we were up at the crack of dawn to dress for duty.

We no doubt looked like a regiment of royal recruits clonking down the road in our army boots. We were the first British nurses to arrive, and, as such, the first women. Because of our curious outfits, rumour amongst the natives had it that the British army was short of men and had sent its women to fight! We were not permitted to advise them otherwise, and we all had a bit of a chuckle over that one.

Thus elegantly outfitted, we ate our Christmas dinner of bully beef and biscuits in the officers' mess. It didn't look or feel like Christmas, but we sang our hearts out in carol after carol that evening, silently thankful to be still alive.

The men told us, with grave faces, that our large, black boots were quite popular with the natives. We were warned not to walk alone to and from work because the Arabs might kill us for our boots. We kept a close watch on our boots and looked suspiciously at anyone talking about the boots or offering to polish them for us. We soon found out, much to our embarrassment, that the joke was on us. I would have been overjoyed if someone *had* pinched my boots. Sometimes my feet were so hot I thought the boots were on fire, and I envied the Arabs their sandals.

The American survivors' replacement uniforms were flown out immediately, but we wore these army-issue outfits for three months, if one can imagine that. The worst thing about them, despite their heavy weight and uncomfortable feeling, was the lack of manoeuvrability they allowed us for the delicate work we had to do. And, even though it was wartime, we also felt that we looked unfeminine. Of course, as the war progressed and we got busier, we had precious little time to worry about our appearance.

Our initial instructions were to set up the first hospital for troops who were already fighting in North Africa and their reinforcements just now arriving. We were the 95th General Base Hospital, set up to follow the invasion of North Africa. Although we had lost precious time during the torpedoing of the Strathallan, all our equipment was here, so we were on duty almost immediately.

Soon after we were established in the hospital on the outskirts of Algiers, but not quite ready for a crowd of wounded, we received some unexpected patients. Many of the crew off the Royal Navy destroyers which had rescued people from the Strathallan were brought in to us for treatment. The ships had run into trouble not long after dropping us at Oran. While we were all sorry to hear about that, we were tickled pink to return now the kindness of those men who had saved our lives. We shared many more stories and a lot of laughter with them, and there were some tearful goodbyes when they were sent home or returned to duty.

Even in the heat of battle and the horror of war there were some bright spots. The day after our arrival in Algiers, our commanding officer decided to transfer about 30 of us from our orphanage abode to a nearby former harem. The interior was exquisite, with rich mosaic floors so shiny they almost sparkled reflecting off the high ceilings. The harem was built around a large communal centre space surrounded by tiny rooms and toilet facilities. It was so luxurious that we wondered why we had been singled out for this special attention. We soon found out.

It was rumoured that a number of high-ranking Nazi officers were in the area searching for a hideout and it was thought they were planning to hide in the harem. Apparently, we were supposed to foil them by taking up residence there. We didn't ask, just followed orders – sometimes with quizzical expressions and raised eyebrows!

The author of the following verse is unknown, but we were told that the writer was most likely the father of a Q.A. we had known, one of the casualties of the Strathallan. I believe she was in Peebles with us and that her father was in the armed forces also. The writer was obviously aware of the conditions we were faced with, including the temporary loss of our uniforms!

Not in the heat and fury of the fight
Nor crawling stealthily, nerves taut, at night
With blood white-hot, fierce passions all aflame
A cruel folk to seek a dangerous game.
Though close at hand may be at times too near,
The Q.A. does her job, forgets her fear.

Although in battledress, a woman still,
With gentleness combined with strongest will,
Mind and body on a mission spent,
To tend and succour those whom war has rent,
With fingers deft, skilful mind alert,
The Q.A. does her job, relieves the hurt.

Not prominent in headlines, rolls of honour,
For rarely are distinctions showered upon her,
Nor in spectacular displays of might
In which a fickle public takes delight.
But Britain's warriors, in their hearts enshrined,
The Q.A., who to them with glory shines.

I knew lots of Q.A.s to whom I would very quickly have given a medal.

January 1943 found us on duty in Algiers in a big way, with the North African campaign in progress. We were part of what was known as the First Army. Our hospital was becoming more established now; the French gendarmes had been replaced by our own British guards and we were into a regular routine. Algiers was, apparently, the nerve centre of the North African campaign, and everywhere there was activity.

We were on duty most of the time, but the long hours couldn't eliminate the wonderful camaraderie amongst the staff. The uncrushable spirit of our gallant, wounded boys made everything worthwhile. We had a lot of wounded men who needed good conditions.

The converted museum was in rough shape, and our Royal Engineers were working on improving general conditions inside the hospital. They were really terrific at fixing walls and floors and hooking up equipment. It was amazing how quickly things improved.

Outside the hospital, the filth, squalor and absence of sanitation took away any preconceived ideas of the glamour of Africa. Everywhere underfoot there was a thick grey mud, and in that one respect we were almost glad to have men's battledress to wear. We assumed that this was the worst time of year and hoped that things would improve. They did.

Algiers – Spring 1943

The months passed quickly and spring in Algiers was now upon us. Although the war brought death and destruction, spring welcomed in life, beauty and hope. Not that we had much of a chance to appreciate whatever beauty there might have been around us, as we were rushed off our feet tending to our patients. The War Office in Britain had finally replaced most of the belongings we had lost with the ship, and the shipment finally reached us in early March. We were now outfitted in the familiar Q.A. uniform, and things were once again in order.

The fighting had moved further up the coast and was claiming more lives. The stream of wounded soldiers continued. Our large hospital was functioning well, but the demand for more beds necessitated expansion by the fastest and most convenient means possible. That meant erecting large, billowy, canvas tents on the grounds. Working under the canvas was a nice change, although it was hectic at times transporting supplies from the main structure.

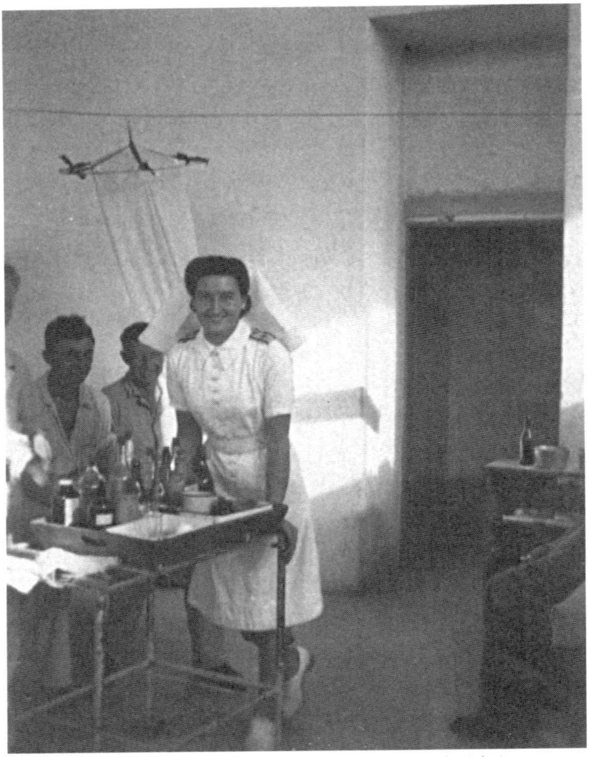

G. Aikens at 95th General Base Hospital, Algiers. Summer Q.A./R. working uniform.

There were a few drawbacks to having our patients in tents, of course. While in Algiers we had two siroccos – hot, dry, dust-laden winds from the desert to the south. Sand landed like fine rain and filtered its way into everything, even the wounds, and the heat was extreme. Dressing our patients' wounds cleanly was a real battle.

Our off-duty time depended entirely on the battles up front, so if the fighting was particularly fierce and the casualties were pouring in, we were on the go constantly from dawn well into the depths of night. But when there was a lull, we took full advantage of it and went exploring.

As we no longer had armed escorts tagging along with us everywhere, our adventuring was a little easier. We quite often would sign out for a couple of hours, hop up on one of those natty army jeeps and head to the core of Algiers to look around.

This central city of gently bending palm trees and vibrant floral shrubbery was breathtakingly beautiful and seemed to consist of only the most elaborate buildings. Tiers of white structures ascended the hills above the bay while the faces of the mosques of the Kasbah shone upon the city. As was the case with a number of other buildings, their facades were much more pleasing than their interiors. It was almost as if the architects had begun elaborately on the outside, planning to work their way inside and do the same, but run out of time, inclination or resources to continue as they had begun.

Having taken a few trips into the main part of the city, we no longer stared, unaccustomed, at the Arab women robed and veiled so that only dark, inquisitive eyes stared back at us. We felt quite comfortable wandering around looking at the diversity of wares which the stores offered.

There were plenty of sizable department stores in the city, all run by the French; their shopkeepers, fears of confiscation of their remaining goods dispelled, were rapidly opening up their shops and an assortment of Arab silver jewellery, leather, woodcraft and silks could be obtained at what we thought were fabulous prices. Perfumes, cosmetics and fruits were both inexpensive and plentiful. Later on in the summer many beauty salons opened up for business. We allowed ourselves this indulgence once in a while, even if the style only lasted for a few hours before wind, sand, dust and our nursing caps put an end to it!

There seemed to be no clearly defined dawn or dusk in this country, but perhaps that was because we worked such long hours that one day dissolved into the next. The cool, early morning came quickly and then, almost without warning, the gentle misty evening enveloped the countryside and our little hospital community. Quite often on the way back to our accommodation we could discern the faint outlines on the hillside of shepherds and their sheep, and sometimes as we lay in our cots we could hear the muted strains of some haunting Arab melody. At about 60°F, the nights were pleasant. After a long, tiring shift, it was nice to be able to sleep comfortably.

On the Ambulance Train – April 1943

Q.A.s from the base hospitals were always being posted temporarily to other area units, mostly ambulance trains. April of 1943 found me posted to a hospital train along with another Q.A. from the base hospital in Algiers. We had trouble finding the hospital train we had been assigned to, but finally, after chasing around Algiers in an ambulance for the elusive locomotive "SS102," we found it at Rouiba, a military siding out in the wilds.

Ambulance trains provided medical care to wounded soldiers while en route to base hospitals like the one in Algiers. The trains travelled close to the rear of combat areas to collect patients who were brought to the train by ambulance from battlefield casualty clearance stations.

The ambulance trains were shunted, for various reasons, into areas of railway stations far from the main line and were usually shunted with all of the hospital crew on board! Sometimes the lot of us would be shunted way out into the countryside on an abandoned line and work and live there a while until we got orders to move again.

Because of the great cloud of secrecy always hovering, we never knew where we were going. Sometimes we got information by listening to snippets of conversation, hushed whispers over cups of tea or coffee. Quite often we just guessed, and the odd time the reason would appear, such as when extra staff arrived. We went everywhere and

SS102 hospital train

did most things by order from military headquarters, and we were moved like chess pieces from one place to another.

We discovered that this train we were on, the SS102, which was carrying British troops, was staffed by French officers – three men and two nurses. We spoke English, they spoke French and both sides felt uncomfortable with one another. We might have expected this as Algeria had been heavily settled by French immigrants after being colonized by France in the mid-nineteenth century.

We also felt vulnerable, as we had no senior medical officer on board. Fortunately we did have a few Royal Army Medical Corpsmen, which helped, but basically we couldn't believe that the authorities had done this to us. An ambulance train usually carried two British medical officers, two Q.A.s, five or six Royal Army Medical Corps orderlies and a British cook. Our cooks were at first not even allowed in the kitchen by the French officers!

I shared a compartment with the other Q.A. on the train. Uneasy with the French cooking and lifestyle which seemed to predominate, we used that tiny compartment as dining room, bedroom and sitting room. The one washroom in our carriage, which was fortunately close by our room, was for all 48 staff and crew on board! C'est la guerre!

No sooner had we settled into our carriage and our little compartment than we had to pick up stakes and move into temporary accommodations due to bedbugs. The carriage was upholstered, thus providing a great home for the little creatures and creating a nightmare for us. We figured that the problem must prevail throughout the train, and we expected we would be hearing stories from the rest of the crew. But our carriage seemed to be the only one infested.

As nurses we'd had to deal with bedbugs before, especially in district nursing in the poorer homes of Sheffield, so we knew the routine well. But that didn't make dealing with the situation any more pleasant. We had been told that the French trains were known for their cleanliness and, given that accolade, we were particularly offended to find bedbugs. I made a mental note to raise the topic with whomever had given me that bit of misinformation.

That incident behind us and my friend and I settled into alternate quarters, an easy routine was soon established. Life on the hospital train, especially with a completely French-speaking crew, was a truly novel experience. After a few unavoidable clashes, mostly language differences but also medical differences affecting the patients, we finally established a solid friendship with the "crew français." The medicine chef, as he was called, spoke German and French but no English. His assistant, known as "la gestionnaire," something like a quartermaster, I suppose, was an active, intelligent man with an infectious personality whom we liked immediately. We called him Peter, and under our tutelage he soon spoke a fair amount of English. While we waited for the ambulances to arrive with their wounded passengers, he entertained us with catchy French tunes.

Our food aboard the train was cooked by the chef de cuisine, a somewhat obese man who usually wore baggy black pantaloons, a starched white shirt and a small sailor cap. He exuded, not unpleasantly, the aroma of garlic. Every time we went into the kitchen to see if we could find a morsel of something English to eat we were told emphatically, non!

The diet of the French crew consisted of large amounts of artichokes, olive oil, garlic, brown bread, omelette, frogs' legs, snails and, of course, copious amounts of wine. Our favourite afternoon fare of tea and biscuits was simply not on the menu. We were told to expect our rations of English food on the next ambulance at the next station and until then we would have to be patient. As the water was suspect and we were not allowed to drink wine, we existed for the next two days on brown bread and a peculiar hot liquid which we were advised was indeed tea.

We soon took aboard a couple of new recruits, also French-speaking. We hadn't been looking forward to their arrival, and the other Sister and I kept muttering under our breath about all these foreign-speaking people on board and where were the rest of our English-speaking staff? But although we hadn't planned on establishing anything but a strict working relationship with them, the other Q.A. and I found that we got along extremely well with the two French Sisters who arrived. As one spoke English fluently, we could all communicate quite well. She would translate for the other, who understood only snippets of English, we devised a crude form of sign language which we all found humorous.

Soukahras, Algeria – May 1943

By now we were on a regular schedule. Our mission was to transport about 230 casualties from Soukahras in the east to Algiers every third day. The journey was about 360 miles. Those travels from Algiers to Soukahras were long and extremely hot, but colourful, and we saw this part of North Africa at both its best and its worst.

It was fascinating, when our train stopped at various places to fill up with water, to see the local children in their rags and tatters. Sometimes wee girls, tattooed and adorned with silver anklets, earrings and bracelets, would clamour around the train, their skinny, sun-drenched arms outstretched towards us. They were all shouting in unison, in their little acquired English, "Biscuit Johnny, chewing gum, chocolat," obviously influenced by the American forces.

They were often laden with baskets filled with fruits or eggs. Although our hearts went out to these children, we were forbidden to buy any of their wares. Farther along our route we passed women prodding their weary mules, the vital labourers of the country. We also saw many white horses and once or twice glimpsed a camel.

On one occasion we stopped in a siding called Tuilleries, a lovely valley in the hills through which meandered a brilliant, narrow stream just deep enough in parts for fishing and swimming. As usual, the British army had more rules and regulations than the French, so although our French companions did, we could not venture near the river. We consoled ourselves by remembering we had so much work to do that there really wasn't time for bathing and relaxing. More privately, we were scared

SS102 at right, on the siding at Tuilleries

to get off the train, not knowing the countryside and the places where enemies might lurk.

The work on the train was tiring but satisfying, although at times I wondered exactly what it was we were all doing in this war. One particularly warm spring evening I was going through the carriage checking on the men and tending to their injuries; some required more attention and medication than others for their pain. A faint voice from a top bunk nearby whispered something like "vassa." My head was almost next to the whispering soldier's now; he was deathly pale. His light blue eyes looked appealingly into mine and he repeated, "vassa." I just couldn't get it.

Then one of the men in another stretcher leaned over and said, "He wants water, Sister; he's a Gerry, I think." I stood paralysed. My father had been killed in World War I by the Germans and now here was this German asking me for water. How could this POW have become mixed up in the train with our British and Allied soldiers?

As the other patients looked on in silence, sensing my unease, I gave him a teaspoon of water from a glass and then went to the medicine chef, who could speak German, to ascertain whether the patient had internal injuries which would forbid the taking of anything by mouth. I returned and spoon-fed the German soldier with water until he finally lay back and closed his eyes.

When everything was settled I retired to my compartment with a cup of tea and thought how stupid war was. I remembered a patient in Algiers who suffered from shellshock. The psychiatrist believed that if the men could talk about their troubles in the war it would help them to recover. They were using sodium pentothal, the truth serum, as they called it. That boy in Algiers could not have been any more than 20, and I sat with him through his treatment and listened to his story.

There had obviously been severe fighting and this boy had been using a machine gun. Under attack, while most of his buddies had been killed, he went on shooting madly. Suddenly, an enemy soldier was right under the barrel of the boy's gun. The boy shot him. He said, "It was either him or me, Sister. What was I supposed to do?" He cried like a baby for an hour or more before he drifted off into a deep sleep.

But his words kept replaying in my mind, "I could see him Sister, he was just a boy like me and I killed him." Having come face to face with the "enemy" just a few moments ago, I knew what he meant. The next morning, after the train had wound its way back through the countryside and into Algiers, we finally unloaded our patients, including the POW, who would now be placed where he belonged.

We often had to stop for quite a while in Soukahras on our regular trips there from Algiers. Soukahras seemed, on first impression, a dirty, dusty Arab village, badly bombed and in shambles. And so we were very surprised to find that it possessed a cosmopolitan hotel, the Orientie, which, luckily for us, was still standing. Here we were allowed to buy a frugal meal, mineral water and a treat of ice cream. We met up with some old friends and watched the passing parade of British, French and American officers. Soukahras was apparently a meeting place for everyone passing through from east to west. Some of those were now going on four days' rest leave after working nonstop for six months.

On one such stopover in Soukahras, the other Q.A. and I joined a couple of the officers and visited an Arab regiment in town, of which one of the officers was in charge. While there we had a chance to see a bit of the local entertainment. A delicate Arab girl, no more than 10 years old, danced to her native music, moving rhythmically to the beat. There was almost a mystique surrounding the dance and the people watching; the whole atmosphere inside the large tent was magical and entrancing.

The Q.A. with whom I was working on the train was from Scotland, a sweet person and a terrific nurse. She had fallen in love with a Royal Engineering officer in Algiers who had come to Soukahras. They planned to meet here, get engaged later on, and then buy an engagement ring here on their return. She and I were deployed to different destinations after our next trip out, and I didn't return to Soukahras for quite a while. I didn't get a chance to talk to her before she left, and I wondered if she and her fiancé got married finally.

This part of North Africa was more of an invasion area with the main battle areas in and around the city of Tunis. The Germans had taken Tunis, but they had been driven out by the British and their allies around the first week of May 1943.

In the United States it was believed that most of the fighting in this battle had been done by the Americans. In fact, even though the campaign couldn't have been won without American troops and equipment, the whole operation had been British. From the start of the Tunisian campaign to its finish, the Americans had never amounted to more than a quarter of the troops.

In Soukahras, Tunisians continued to celebrate in the streets even though the victory was a few days old. There was shouting and singing and people were handing out cigarettes. Dusty, unshaven soldiers were being hugged by grown men loaded with flowers. Soldiers were everywhere and refugees from the Axis were emerging from cellars where they had been hidden for months.

The French on our ambulance train were also making merry. Our train came alive with voices swelled in song and the French national anthem, the Marseillaise, could be heard from one end of the train to the other as the wine flowed freely. We Brits soon got into it too, singing our renditions of "God Save the King" and "There Will Always Be an England." We weren't overzealous, though, because to us it was only a small victory and we knew there was much more war ahead.

POW trains passed our Soukahras railroad-siding location continually, loaded with German and Italian prisoners of war guarded by French and British police. The majority of the prisoners looked rather nonchalant. Our train, which made regular stops along the route for water supplies as well as for security reasons, pulled up one evening right beside a POW train. We had only been stopped there for about half an hour when we heard a lot of shouting and footsteps echoing everywhere.

Once our train got moving again we learned that some enterprising prisoners had cut a hole in the floor of the POW train next to ours. Two had escaped. Because our train was empty at the time, it was thought that the escapees might have hidden on it and so our train was given a thorough search. No escapees were found and we went on our way, although a few of us, myself included, remained wary.

The next day our train pulled into the small coastal town of Philippeville to collect patients, and on the return journey we stayed in the town of Constantine for train repairs. We hadn't noticed anything wrong with our train and so suspected that the search was still on for the two escapees. Constantine was a very old French-influenced Arab town, spread above and around a spectacular craggy gorge. An immense, solidly constructed bridge spanned the spacious gorge. We took the opportunity to tour the famous canyon and visit the old Roman baths and swimming pools along the sides of the lower canyon, where old Roman coins and curios were still being recovered.

While Tunis and Soukahras and other areas were celebrating, the battle was continuing elsewhere. The famous Eighth Army was locked in battle about 30 miles from Sousse around Enfidaville on the coast across the sea from Sicily. It was now May 25, 1943. News was always scant, but we knew that something was going haywire because

Part of the gorge at Constantine. A Spitfire had recently flown up the canyon and under this bridge to escape enemy aircraft, causing great excitement locally.

instead of heading from Constantine back to Algiers, as usual, we were now scheduled to return to Soukahras.

Upon our arrival there we found that we would be travelling for at least another day to a place called Sidi Smyle, almost to Tunis. We passed many battle sites and war-scarred country and got a good idea of the type of land our men were faced with. It must have been rough going. We were stopped in Sidi Smyle for three days and our train was staged at the side of an airfield. We were to supervise the loading of patients from hospital planes onto our ambulance train.

In the midst of that task, the staff and patients were fortunate to enjoy a little bit of wartime entertainment.

Setif, between Algiers and Soukahras. The railway tracks ran over the viaduct.

Touring field shows where famous people like Bob Hope and his entourage would entertain the troops, often set up in the surrounding fields. Whatever the ground cover – sand, grass, gravel or mud – up would go the stage and anywhere from 100 to 5000 onlookers attended, sitting on chairs, patient beds or stretchers. It didn't matter where we sat, as long as we were entertained for a while and could take our minds off the war.

We weren't expecting any more planeloads of patients for a day or so and could therefore do some more sightseeing. One afternoon a friend and I visited the Dougga ruins in a place called Beja near the hamlet of Teboursouk, not that far from Tunis and the action in Enfidaville. These

Dougga ruins were the magnificently preserved remains of an old Roman city. The typical mosaic floors were everywhere and one could easily discern the remnants of what had once been an amphitheatre, bars, dining halls and baths. After visiting the ruins we used the remaining time to tour the French military diesel trains, which we learned could carry about 40 patients.

After our few days in Sidi Smyle, we travelled back to Soukahras where we picked up 200–300 patients to be transported back to the base hospital in Algiers. The fall of Tunis had temporarily suspended the use of the French hospital trains and for this reason we were returning to the base in Algiers.

It was on that return journey that I had the scare of my life. We had left Soukahras and were travelling through a sort of dry wilderness area. Our train consisted of about five carriages with the engine at the front, staff car and patient carriages in the middle and the caboose at the rear. I was in the caboose. I stepped out the back door of the caboose onto the platform to shake out a blanket and the carriage door slammed behind me, locking shut.

I couldn't catch anyone's attention and had no way of stopping the train. I knew that these old trains had a sort of mudguard along the edge and a rail along the windows; I had seen Arabs get free rides on similar trains and wondered if I dared walk along the outside to the other end of the carriage. The door at the other end was always open.

I couldn't look at the locked door, debating my dilemma, for too long because there were sick people on board in need of attention. And it would soon be growing dark. I started to inch my way along the outside edge of the train. I didn't dare look behind or below me because the train tracks were perched on a ridge which plummeted sharply down into the desert below.

The train was only travelling at a snail's pace, about 10 miles per hour, which made my task a little easier to tackle. About halfway along, I peered into a window and saw a patient lying awake, his head propped up on his pillow, looking straight out the window. He must have seen me. He would think he was dreaming, I supposed, or perhaps he thought that walking along the outside of a moving train was a part of Q.A. duties? My hands were stiff with tension and then I nearly lost my footing and slipped as the train suddenly swayed around a sharp curve.

When I had almost reached the haven at the caboose's other end, I saw that two men sat on the step in the opening where the caboose and next carriage joined. They were in uniforms with a funny-looking headdress. Although the uniforms were intriguing, it was the long, curved knives, with very sharp-looking edges, that caught my attention. The knives were just sitting at the sides of these men, the sun's rays winking off them every so often.

Well, I didn't care, these two men would just have to kill me then. As I approached them quietly, taking in a deep breath, I was prepared for the worst. But nothing happened. They looked perplexed when they glanced up and saw me standing before them, but they simply rose to let me pass as though nursing Sisters came that way all the time.

Safely back inside, I didn't breathe a word of my escapade to anyone until much later, when I casually asked someone about the two men on the step. I was told that they were Gurkhas, part of a crack Nepalese fighting force that was part of the British army in India, very tough and extremely loyal. If they'd had the slightest inclination that I was the enemy, they could have sliced me in half with those huge knives of theirs. On the other hand, if they had thought I was in any kind of trouble they would have been the first to rescue me. A comforting thought.

They were used to seeing the Q.A.s with the troops and so wouldn't have thought it unusual to see me, and as they preferred the cooler air outside the train, perhaps they thought I was outside for the same reason.

The Gurkhas were headed into Algiers with the rest of us. I am not sure why they were going to Algiers and I couldn't find out. In Algiers they vanished, uniforms, knives and all.

A Glimpse of Tunis

After about a month back in the familiarity of the base hospital in Algiers, I was posted, along with eight other Sisters, to a general hospital in Sousse. General Montgomery's forces had split into two parts, one branching northward and the other going to Sousse. We were told the Sousse hospital was in an olive grove, which we imagined would be quite beautiful. Our map showed Sousse to be located right on the Mediterranean just below Tunis. We first had to get from Algiers to Tunis and from there we would carry onward to Sousse.

Although our ambulance train had made this journey up and down the coast before, we had been too busy tending to the wounded to see any of the countryside. What we saw en route to Tunis were fields lush with bluebells, poppies, tulips and daisies, marred by the residue of fierce battles. With grief we gazed at the little graves here and there of both British and German soldiers killed in their Tunisian campaign. Everywhere were overturned, charred vehicles, old ammunition and petrol dumps and scenes of recent encampments – burned-out campfires where the boys had most likely made their last "brew up," consumed a meal and shared a few jokes before entering the fray.

While waiting a few hours to change trains at Tunis, we were taken to the Majestic Hotel for lunch. The hotel must have been all the name implies in peacetime, but it had been converted into an officers' mess and was literally crawling with Allied forces. The food was nothing to write home about – thinly sliced Spam on thinly sliced bread with no butter or mayonnaise and some sort of liquid refreshment which had been given the seal of approval by the authorities.

As a few of us toured the city afterwards, we noted that it showed few signs of warfare. The city of Tunis, one of the largest in Africa, had been left virtually unscathed by bombing. The harbour, however, had been the enemy's playground, with docks split apart, hulls of ships lying on top of one another and even a sunken hospital ship partly still above the water with pieces of wreckage bobbing around it.

Settled back in the train again, I stared out at the war-torn land and thought about the men we had lost and those we had waved out of sight, praying for them at the same time. Perhaps because of the chance to reflect upon life in the face of death, war seems to make poets and artists out of men. They were always handing me little bits of poetry and drawings. Some men, not unlike poet Rupert Brooke, who became famous for his writings in World War I, managed to send their writings home. More often, they gave them to us or wrote their verses in our autograph albums.

I remember a young corporal in my ward at the hospital in Algiers who was waiting to return to the U.K. Both of his legs had been amputated. At a loss for activity, yet wanting fulfillment, he had started sketching. I remember him telling me that he had never had a lesson or done anything like this before. We couldn't keep him in paper, and drawing probably saved his sanity. Fortunately he had a wife back home, and he was keeping all his sketches in a box for her.

Another of my patients, a sapper in the Royal Engineers, wrote of the appalling conditions under which the medical officers and nursing Sisters worked. I kept this young man's poetry because it seemed to describe how we all felt. He had never written poetry before, but clearly the fighting in Tunis had left a horrible taste in his mouth.

They sent me to Blighty I think as a test
To see if a change and a few days of rest
Would bring back the brains the climate sent west
While soldiering out there in Tunis.

If I should seem strange and my actions seem queer
And I look like a wandering Jew, never fear,
As I'm perfectly harmless, that's why I came here
After soldiering out there in Tunis.

If I should do things that seem senseless to you,
You'll find there's a method in all things I do.
I'm a marvel at catching flies, fever and flu,
We learn it out there in Tunis.

If you should see me adrift in the street,
With rifle in hand and kitbag at feet,
Just speak to me gently and say it's the heat
Of that damnable country around Tunis.

If whilst in the Strand I am found charging a bus
Or otherwise making a hell of a fuss,
If smashed and squashed up, don't stand there and stare,
For I'm only a madman from Tunis.

There's no disease known that's not thrived in that den
That dries up one's blood and the ink in one's pen,
And earth covers many of England's best men
In that damnable country around Tunis.

Sousse, Tunisia – June 1943

The final leg of our trip from Tunis to Sousse was unpleasant. The country was barren and uninteresting. Travelling facilities were awful, the dampness in the air chilled us and, as food supplies were low, we often felt hungry. We had picked up more Q.A.s in Tunis, some of whom had been in the field units and were now posted to Sousse, so there were many unfamiliar faces in the train. It was midnight when we finally arrived at our destination and, as usual, we were not expected. No one knew anything about us! Our hospital was eight miles away, so we sat on our luggage in the bleakness of the station and awaited transportation.

Finally, ambulances appeared. Apart from transporting patients, ambulances carrying the international Red Cross insignia on top were also used for transporting medical officers and nurses. As soon as the bags were on board, we started out for the hospital. As our vehicle bumped up and down on the potholes and rough sections of the road, I was reminded of riding on the Blackpool Big Dipper, one of our British roller coasters.

We landed shaken and dishevelled, feeling like pieces of our own luggage, at a dark, sandy wasteland at 2:00 a.m. The officer in charge roused the matron who, we found out, had expected us six days ago. She was sympathetic, despite the time of morning, and had someone show us to our sleeping quarters. We got ourselves settled in two empty tents and slept on stretchers, oblivious to whatever might be around us.

Morning put in far too speedy an appearance, and when we glimpsed our surrounding olive grove we almost wished it was still the black of night. Stretches of sand and olive trees, sand and more olive trees, dusty parched-looking tents scattered everywhere, camp beds loosely strung to trees with mosquito netting. Eight o'clock in the morning brought its usual routine for newcomers, after which we went on duty.

The campaign now raging across the narrows in Sicily kept us going flat-out for the next two months, and during that time life seemed a constant struggle. In the daytime, while we were trying to tend to the patients we were pestered by millions of flies, and in the early evening the mosquitos took over. With all the mosquitoes, there was very little malaria. Maybe all those tiny malaria pills had helped. We still had to take precautions, of course, and the flies and the extreme heat necessitated frequent changes of clothing.

Washing became almost a constant ritual. Soap and water were limited, but drying was immediate! As the days passed the heat increased and sleep was at times impossible. We occasionally got a reprieve when cool evening breezes washed over the land, blowing away the mosquitoes with it. Then, sleeping out in the open became an unforgettable experience. We were frequently awakened by low-flying gliders going to the battle area in Sicily. On cots or hammocks outside the tents, we lay on our backs and gazed at the sky. The planes were so low we could see their markings. They weren't enemy planes or that would have been the end of us!

Although the olive groves had not been quite as glamorous as anticipated, we discovered that Sousse was a charming hillside town. Although its harbour had been heavily bombed, the town itself had escaped. Apart from the town, there were the seas and shores around Sousse. The day after we arrived we had been taken by ambulance to a little place by the shore to swim, about seven or eight of us at a time. It was to become a favourite spot. We had been able to find a little structure which had a few rudely constructed benches to sit on and some tables where we could spread out a picnic luncheon and gaze out at the water.

Amidst rubble and ruin, we made the most of swimming in that clear, refreshing water. I remember gleefully joining the rest of the group splashing around one sweltering afternoon. The tide was high on the shore and the waves were lapping gently against the pebbles. I felt wonderful. Afterwards, we sat around sipping lemonade. Some plunged back into the sea. After a few hours, the receding tide revealed a huge bomb crater not far at all from where I had bathed. What a shock I had. As a nonswimmer, I could easily have drowned. From then on, I cooled off close to shore.

On a subsequent visit to our picnic/swimming spot my eyes were opened to a phenomenon I had only heard of. We had purchased a large watermelon from an Arab outside the hospital and brought it with us. We had chopped the fruit into large pieces, hungrily consumed it all, and placed the rinds on the sandy ground until we were ready to leave.

It was incredible. My large discarded rind began moving down the sand, seemingly by itself! Still more amazingly, there were only three or four sizeable black ants underneath the object, carting it away. As I looked around, I noticed this was going on all over the place. The ants were even venturing into the paper bags and spiriting away pieces of peel and skin – single file, perhaps under military influence! After this little episode, we ate our lunches in our little building or a tent before coming down to the shore.

While in Sousse, we met some of the famous "desert rats" of the Eighth Army. They were a British armoured division and one of the finest fighting machines in the Anglo-American forces. The name of their commander, General Bernard Montgomery, stood higher than that of any other officer. They were well educated, young and handsome and were some of the finest soldiers in the world. They sported khaki shorts, shirts, socks and desert boots and usually wore a brightly coloured neckerchief instead of a khaki tie. They had been through everything.

The enemy had first called them desert rats because they would dig holes in the sand, place a few thick, warm blankets at the bottom, crawl in and then cover the holes with camouflage netting so that they were thoroughly hidden. From October 1942 to January 1943 this army had

Temporary home of a "desert rat"

advanced 1500 miles across some of the most inhospitable country in the world. Stationed in Tobruk and El Alamein, in the desert of the Middle East, the Eighth Army had fought a major action at Alamein and captured 30,000 prisoners. This was one of the most important victories of the war. We had heard many stories about the desert rats. It was an honour to meet them.

About two months after our arrival in Sousse, we were all packed and ready to go again. On the September 3, 1943, we sailed from Sousse in a hospital ship called the St. David.

Hospital sometimes ships carried the war wounded from the battle sites to hospital units on land. They were

Hospital ship St. David

the common means of returning seriously wounded soldiers to the U.K.

With some exception, hospital ships were supposed to be safe from bombing. Unfortunately, this wasn't always the case. The St. David later met its doom off the Anzio bridgehead, the scene of heavy fighting in north Italy. We heard the ship had been bombed while collecting patients.

Fate had placed us in south Italy at that time. I had been lucky; others not so.

Italy

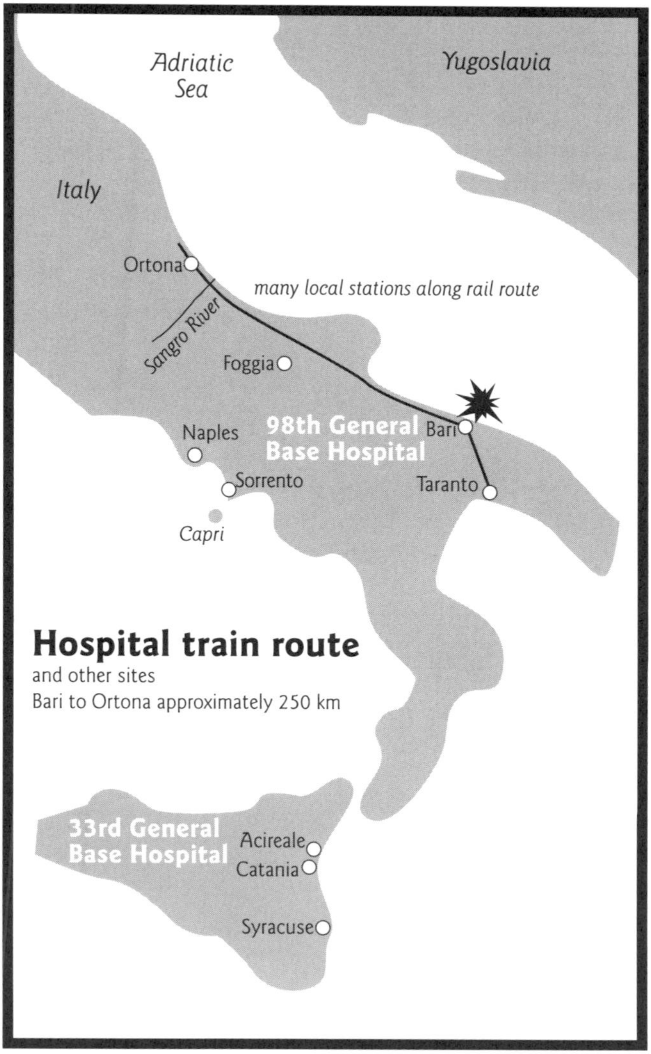
Adriatic Sea
Yugoslavia
Italy
Ortona
many local stations along rail route
Sangro River
Foggia
Naples
98th General Base Hospital
Bari
Sorrento
Taranto
Capri
Hospital train route
and other sites
Bari to Ortona approximately 250 km
33rd General Base Hospital
Acireale
Catania
Syracuse

The 33rd General Base Hospital, Sicily – September 1943

We were told we were going to set up a hospital in Sicily in a port called Syracuse. The St. David sailed smoothly into port with many of us standing at the railing watching as Sicily came into view. We disembarked and were driven to the 33rd General Base Hospital where we were billeted.

After unpacking, we left the grounds of the hospital to wander around the city. What struck us the most was the beauty of the women. Syracusans were kind, gentle people. We liked the city and were prepared to settle in here for a while. Experience should have told us that this was not to be. After only two days we left, travelling up the coast towards Catania.

Even though it had been almost levelled in fierce bombing, the Sicilian city of Catania was one of the prettiest cities I had ever seen. It boasted wide streets and little shops filled with silks, ready-made garments, watches, other delicate jewellery, cosmetics and fruit of every description. After what we had been used to, this was heaven. As we had little or no money, window-shopping became quite the rage.

We did manage to buy a few oddments of cosmetics and other small items that we had not been able to replace since the sinking of the Strathallan. The British Eighth Army had taken control of Catania the previous month, but we saw no sign of armed conflict and wondered where the fighting had been. Our hospital equipment had been lost at sea on the way over from North Africa, and we were not quite sure where in the city we would be stationed. After some delay and a flood of questions, we were finally assigned billets.

What contrasts! Our billets were slum clearance flats which we were initially not too keen about. They seemed to be made of pink cement, built with narrow, winding flights of grey stone steps. But they offered the joy of real bathrooms. There was one on each floor, complete with a shower and running water. We spent entirely too much of our off-duty time in them, and we almost had to book ahead for occupancy!

Our flats were surrounded by refuse dumps, debris and small tumbledown cottages where Sicilian families lived in squalid conditions. Flies and mosquitoes swarmed constantly in greyish clouds. Emaciated women and children, flies crawling around their eyes and ears, came constantly to our doors and windows begging for something to eat. It was heartbreaking. That they were starving was no exaggeration. We gave them the portion of our rations that we could do without. The women proved to be wonderful launderers, and we paid them what we could for keeping our uniforms clean and neatly pressed.

The army took over a building which had originally been a stadium. It smelled of wet wool, manure, stale hay and rotting garbage. "Dear heaven," I thought, "was there nowhere else in this city that could be used as a makeshift hospital?" We had to set about scrubbing and disinfecting the rooms immediately. Luckily, we were never short-handed when it came to cleaning duty. The male members on board always pitched in and helped the Sisters with the work. Our long-lost equipment, known officially as G10-98, had still not been replaced, but we were able to borrow some Italian medical equipment and were soon prepared for the work ahead.

We had no sooner commenced our final mopping up than a batch of extremely wounded patients was brought in. The medication, the needles, intravenous, books and signs on the boxes were printed or marked in languages foreign to us, but we washed the wounded and did the dressings and made our patients warm and comfortable. Not long afterward, the patients were fixed up and in ambulances en route to their next port of call.

In the quiet period that followed, we took the chance to look around the city. Commanding the whole of Catania and a stretch of coast for miles around was a range of mountains including the magnificent Mount Etna, a breathtaking sight looming 10,758 feet into the sky. At times this dormant volcano appeared to be blowing rings with the mist, and often the summit was capped with virgin snow. Each part of the day presented it in a different colour.

Arrangements were made for our unit Sisters and medical officers to climb Etna – those in charge liked us to be kept occupied. I thought I should be able to climb without difficulty. After all, wasn't that what Welsh people did, sing and climb mountains? I had always wanted to climb my native Snowdon in Wales but had never had the opportunity. Permission was granted for transportation to the base of the mountain. We were to go in a rickety bus which gave a very shaky ride. Upon our arrival, we found an old hotel run by a family who cheerfully provided us with sandwiches and cool drinks. We walked around marvelling at the beautiful chestnut trees. And then we climbed.

There was a distinct trail, and we were told by our leaders to go as far as we could and then rest and wait for other people coming back before returning. It was really stiff climbing, and in the increasing cold and lack of oxygen we stopped more and more frequently. Underfoot was dry lava rock, like large gravel, digging into the soles of our boots. There were millions of ladybugs crawling through the lava. It was hard to avoid walking on them; they were like a slow-moving, rust-coloured carpet spread across the rock.

I got farther up the trail than most. A majority managed to reach the observatory, a little landing where we could stop and rest and see the summit a short way further up. Due to thick mist we were forced to retrace our steps to the bus without setting foot on the top of Mount Etna, but the experience had been well worth the climb.

The Sicilians who could went out of their way to shower us with kindness, always wanting to entertain us with food. A group of us was, on one occasion, invited to dine at the home of a well-to-do family. Their dwelling, right at the base of Mount Etna, was magnificent, almost oriental in appearance, with brightly coloured silk wall hangings, elaborate ceilings, thick pile carpets.

Our host and hostess, a middle-aged couple, overwhelmed us with their hospitality. We tried out our school French and what we had picked up in North Africa on the ambulance train, and we seemed able to communicate well enough. We were plied with wines and liqueurs of every description, large juicy watermelons, huge black grapes, a compote of peaches, apples and pears prepared in thick black syrup, almonds and various other sweets. Our host and hostess were so very attentive that, feeling the effects of a few glasses of wine, I began to think about spies and foreign agents. It suddenly occurred to me we might be the victims of some Nazi plot and at this very moment could be drinking poisoned wine. We didn't know any secrets, so they would have been wasting their time and wine.

We woke the next morning to the realities of war and the work to be done. I wasn't the only one who had harboured suspicions, and I think we all felt a little foolish to have suspected our hosts, although I suppose nothing was ever that foolish in wartime. Orders arrived for us to move again, this time not very far. We arrived at a convent in a small place called Acireale overlooking the sea. Half of the building we were to work from was still occupied by the nuns, who were happy to do most of our laundry and sewing.

The Sicilians were excellent needlewomen and did the most exquisite lace and embroidery work. As we wandered through the small cobblestone streets we could see these women in the doorways, their fingers flying deftly with their artistic work.

As we were on hold, waiting to follow the battle wherever it went, we occupied our time taking long walks, picking plump, fresh lemons to send home. We were allowed to bathe in a nearby bay, which like most places along the coast was rugged and rather dangerous, so we did not venture far out or stay too long. Often while we were out walking we would visit the graves of Allied soldiers who had been killed in this last campaign. There were numerous quaint little cafes; we would sit comfortably eating baked walnuts and sipping on Chianti while gazing out at the scenery.

We weren't in Sicily long enough to digest the whole political picture, but the portrait of the Italian dictator, Il Duce, was painted on several of the walls in the town, and the manner in which many of the Sicilians pointed at him while shrugging their shoulders in despair gave one the impression that these people were in the war most reluctantly.

As Catania had shown us, Sicily was a place of very great contrast – rich prosperous homes and businesses, and streets filled with beggars. Some of the beggars were elderly, but, as we had noticed previously on our travels, the majority of them here in Acireale were tiny young ragamuffins, always swatting at the flies crawling around their faces while begging for food and cigarettes.

Since I had imagined this island and the town of Acireale to be a quaint and relaxed little spot, I was surprised to awaken at 5:00 one morning to the muffled noises of the local fishing fleet moving slowly out to sea. From the balcony, I could see hundreds of wee lights bobbing on the waves. About an hour later, a few of us ventured down to the stores and found them all open for business, their proprietors getting an early start on the day just as the fishermen had. They appeared to work without effort and seemed unconcerned about the poverty around them. This was their way of life and they were accustomed to it.

Just when we were getting used to Acireale, we received orders to move again. We knew there was a battle raging in Italy and figured that was where we were headed. Sure enough, we learned that we were now headed back to Catania where we would board a waiting ship and follow the troops over to the Italian mainland. We assembled in Catania, only 25 of us this time.

Just before we were to leave for Italy, one of our Q.A.s received bad news. Her husband had been reported missing and was thought to be a POW in a Japanese concentration camp. She was terribly upset and could have returned to the U.K. to await further word on her husband's fate, but she said there was no point, since she had joined the army in hopes of being in the same war zone as her husband. They had only been married a few months before her husband had left for overseas. She continued bravely through Italy with the rest of us, hoping all the time to receive more news of her husband.

We sailed out of Catania in another converted P&O liner that was already quite full of other officers and nursing Sisters joining us from other areas and from ships which had been the target of enemy fire. Everywhere on board were groups of people talking about their experiences; most of the stories were survivor stories.

One which was particularly distressing was that of a Q.A. on a hospital ship that had been torpedoed. The crew had managed to get some of the people out through a large smashed porthole. Although they made a valiant effort to push her through, this Q.A. was just too fat; there was no choice but to leave her there. I felt the tears well up. In peacetime or on land this would have been humorous, but this story was devoid of humour. The war and the sea had no mercy, and stories like this one brought that point home to us all.

I thought again about the Strathallan and the cabins we had passed on the way to the lifeboats. The picture of cabin doors stuck shut due to the listing of the ship was vivid in my mind, and I could still hear the anguished shouts and pleas of those people on the other side of the cabin doors. In a secure hospital situation, in peacetime, there were always emergencies, but with knowledge and experience we were routinely successful in handling them. In wartime, however, we were all too frequently faced with horrors we could do nothing about.

We were all so busy talking about our experiences and tragedies at sea, that we didn't at first notice the lack of momentum of the ship. There were a few wild-faced officers dashing about, but no information coming from any of them. We didn't seem to be close to anything, no land in sight. It sounded as if the engine had stopped and the old girl just seemed to be circling aimlessly in the open sea. This continued for a day or so, and as usual rumours were rampant. I managed to contain my nervousness, hoping with all my heart that this wasn't to be the Strathallan all over again. Finally we were told we would be turning around and heading back to the closest port.

We landed a short while later in the southeastern Italian port of Brindisi. We were soon informed that a British destroyer sailing ahead of us had struck a mine and been blown up in the harbour of Bari, the port city for which we had been destined. "Not a bad reason for turning around," I thought, shivering just a little. I thought about fate and how it really had been on my side all along.

Upon receiving clearance, we were back on our way, this time via road. A convoy of army trucks bumped us around hairpin bends from Brindisi to Bari, a huge seaport on the Adriatic opposite Yugoslavia.

98th General Base Hospital, Bari – November 1943

By October 1943 the German and Italian armies had been defeated in North Africa and in Sicily, and the Allied line had been straightened across southern Italy from Salerno to Bari. By the time we arrived there, Bari was under Allied control with the Allies advancing north. Bari had now become the major port for supplying the Eighth Army, a fact of which the enemy was well aware.

We were on duty immediately in Bari as part of the 98th General Base Hospital which had been set up in a very large, unfinished multi-building complex known as the Polyclinic. Built by the Italians and expropriated by the Allied Forces, the complex housed laboratories, an X-ray department, a pharmacy, an officers' mess, a chapel, the quartermaster's stores and a few other buildings. Surrounding the complex was a huge ring of hut-like residences housing guards and sentries. The roadway ushering the ambulances from the battlefields led right into the midst of the little hospital community. It was an ideal location, very near the harbour, railway and city. The flat roofs, which were easily accessible, commanded magnificent views of Bari Harbour.

The clinic housed probably about 5000 people at a time, all transient except for the staff.

South African, New Zealand and Indian units worked together here, and, up to the time of our arrival, the New Zealand Sisters had been setting up the hospital. What a nice group of people they were. Like us, they had no idea where they would be going next, although they suspected they would be heading back to the Middle East. Despite our varied nationalities, we had one common concern, the treatment of the wounded soldiers.

We were all on duty together to receive the survivors of a large minesweeper which had been blown up in the harbour. At that point it really didn't matter what language was spoken. We nursed many of these wounded naval men back to health only to receive them again a few weeks later as the result of a more ghastly disaster.

It was four days before we established our sleeping quarters, and once again we had bedbugs. We couldn't understand it. This was a large outbuilding which had been used very little, and the particular room in which about 10 of us slept had never been used. We were being bitten at night only, which was frustrating because we needed our sleep.

Some of our windows had no glass, and because mosquitos were still around and biting, we had suspended mosquito netting from the ceiling by hooks and tucked it in all around the mattresses. The hooks were connected to the netting by a narrow flat piece of wood inside the netting. We searched every morning before going on duty and found nothing, but our bites were definitely not mosquito bites.

Two of us decided to do some detective work. The alarm clock rang at 1:00 a.m. I switched on my flashlight instantly and was almost sick. I didn't dare move, but must have let out a shout or a cry, for suddenly there was commotion all around me. Everyone was up and pointing to the netting. Climbing up towards the top of my netting, and that of the bed beside me and the one beside that, and behind the piece of wood inside our netting tents, were hundreds of horrible bedbugs scurrying from the light.

We discovered that they hid in the wood by day. At night they descended upon us, and as morning came they stole silently away to their wood homes. The mosquito netting we were using had been stored after leaving Catania, so we had no idea where or how we had picked up these awful and unwelcome creatures. Everything was immediately fumigated. Some of our scars remained with us forever, a reminder of the unexpected experiences of war.

A Letter Home

We had been here about a month now and I was once again on night duty. It was chilly and unpleasant but fairly quiet with only the occasional moan or cry from one of the men. My shift lasted from 8:00 p.m. until 8:00 the next morning. Two medical officers, about five orderlies, another Q.A. and I had about 90 patients to look after. They were all more or less stable and most were waiting to return by boat to the U.K. or other countries.

I had time to write my mother and sent the letter off the next morning. I soon learned from Mother that a friend of hers had listened to the letter being read and insisted it go in the local paper. It was printed as follows and copies were saved for my return to the U.K.:

SOMEWHERE IN ITALY
Hospital Life Through the Eyes of a Nurse

A glimpse of life in Italy from an unusual angle, that of a hospital at the "front," is contained in an interesting letter recently received by a correspondent from a friend who is one of the Q.A.I.M.N.S./R. Sisters serving with the Army there. The letter reads thus:

I am writing this at 2 a.m., somewhere in Italy. It is extremely cold tonight, and having got all my 90 patients settled down comfortably and warm here I sit in front of a little oil stove with a blanket wrapped around my knees and the cardigan my mother knitted for me round my shoulders – I wish I hadn't lost that beautiful woolly grey cape in the ship …

The kettle of water is almost boiling, having been on two and one-half hours, and when it does I shall make myself a cup of tea, and if any of my patients are lying awake I usually give them one too.

I wish I could take you around this hospital – it really is most impressive. The building itself is jerry-built and flimsy. Interior walls are blue, which go very well with our blue blankets, white sheets and black bed frames. The patients wear grey pyjamas, and when allowed to sit up, have red shoulder capes:

> they have dark blue dressing gowns when allowed to walk about.
>
> While travelling around you hear many different languages and see various coloured skins – I think we have every nationality here except Japanese.
>
> The whole of the medical staff, of course, is in khaki, and we have Indian orderlies – actually there is a special Indian section. Here and there you will find an Indian guard standing smartly to attention, fixed bayonet in hand, and wearing that elaborate headdress of theirs. He is guarding the wounded prisoners of war. Then you have the grey and scarlet "Q.A.s" (nurses) dashing around looking very cheerful yet wondering how on earth they are going to get the work done. Here and there the few Red Cross people we have are dealing with the library, etc. … then you would, maybe, see a padre giving his last blessing or communion to a dying hero, and you quickly pass on with a tear in your eye.
>
> Any hour of the day you would find corridors strewn with stretchers on which were patients either just arriving after a long weary journey looking dirty, tired and ill, or those just going to a base hospital after having wounds redressed, operated on or generally made clean and fit for their next journey, probably to the U.K., which will take them out of danger for a while or for good. Outside, the grounds are lined with buff-coloured ambulances painted with the Red Cross, and at various spots two flags fly – the Union Jack and the Red Cross …

Bari was a large city with a few theatres and myriad shops. We had minuscule personal property, and it was always a treat to buy a little something. I don't recall receiving salary, although we must have, I suppose, and most of mine would have gone to my mother, as I sent it directly home to my bank in the U.K. Our food, clothing, and accommodation were provided, our socializing and relaxation were done in the officers' mess and social gatherings were attended in uniform, so there was really little need for money or any other type of material possession.

There was still a war on and the Q.A.s' work seemed to continue forever, but we enjoyed some socializing and grew close to many people; some of us had stayed together since the beginning. There were some romances too.

Marie, one of the sweetest, most delightful nurses one could ever meet married a young sergeant she had met six months earlier, and it was my first wedding ever. Marie had been with us all since the Strathallan, although she had not been at Peebles. She and her fiancé were from the same city in the U.K., but hadn't met until the war had thrown them together. They were married in a little hospital chapel on the base, and as all in attendance were in uniform, it was quite a wonderful sight to behold.

Our original survivor group from the Strathallan had dwindled as many of the Sisters had been posted to different areas and units. We heard that one of our Q.A. Sisters had died recently in Naples. We never did find out what had happened to her, but she couldn't have been more than 26. We never heard any more of Margaret Bourke-White, the Life Magazine photographer who had been on our lifeboat.

The Bari Raid – December 2, 1943

It was late afternoon. I was scheduled for night duty later on, but as I had promised to write a letter for one of my patients to his girlfriend, I went to see him before my shift began. The navy chap for whom I had begun writing the letter had a tiny anteroom to himself because of eye injuries. We never knew what sort of buildings we would find to put our patients in, but private rooms were rare.

I was sitting with my patient, writing as he dictated to me. Everything seemed to have quieted down. We were not busy, but we were expecting a train convoy at 5:00 the next morning and had finished all preparations for it. There was also an air evacuation from the hospital to take place about the same time. This young man had lost his sight in a mine disaster and should have been on the morning flight to the U.K., but due to another injury, the medical officers didn't think he was quite ready to travel. I believe he was Canadian, and I recall he had a package of lifesavers. The patients often received care packages from home via the Red Cross and this chap had found lifesavers in his box of goodies. I think he could sense that I was curious about the candy with the hole in the middle, so he offered me one. I thought it delicious.

About 6:00 p.m., while I was writing, I could hear gunfire in the distance, which was strange, as the war had supposedly moved further up the coast. Curious, another Q.A. and I decided to try to see where the gunfire was coming from. I told my patient I would be back shortly, and the other Sister and I donned tin helmets and cloaks and ventured stealthily, like a couple of spies, up to the flat roof. There was definitely something happening; the barrage was becoming intense over the harbour, and within an hour the whole place was a blazing inferno. Some of our staff were down by the waterfront seeing to evacuation arrangements for patients going to the U.K. by ship the next day, and we hoped they were alright.

As we lay flat on our stomachs, peering over the sight below us, a powerful explosion suddenly shattered what we thought must have been every window in the building. It was, we decided, time to get back downstairs. Brushing off shards of glass that had landed on us, we gingerly descended the steps, crunching glass. The power was off. No one seemed to have been injured by the flying glass and it didn't appear to be sharp to walk on. The scraping of glass particles being swept away from the main thoroughfare by the orderlies brought on a flood of apprehension, because we knew that with disaster would come the patients.

It wasn't long before the influx of wounded began and I never did finish that letter for my patient. The rumours circulating were all the same – a lone bomber had managed to score a direct hit. Seventeen ships of the Allied forces had been hit. The terrific vibration of the ammunition ships exploding was what had turned our hospital into a glass shambles, but at least it was still standing. We supposed that the ships could not have been too heavily loaded with ammunition, or else we wouldn't have been alive to think about it.

We worked by the dim glow of hurricane lamps. I can remember at one point fixing an intravenous by the light of a single match held by the orderly in front of a heavy screen to prevent the draughts from blowing out the light. While the bitter December wind forced its way in through our makeshift window coverings, we found we had hot running water for the first time. Nothing short of a miracle.

We worked long into the night and early morning. Intravenous bottles were dripping from every third bed and corridors were crammed with patients for whom we could find no accommodation. We were soon receiving patients via the operating theatre, patients with bilateral amputation of legs still wearing their life belts.

The work of the often-overlooked Royal Army Medical Corps orderlies and stretcher-bearers was admirable. They were marvellous, carrying patients in, transferring them to different wards, making hot drinks and keeping us in cups of tea for the next two days and nights. They worked alongside us nonstop, keeping up a cheerful banter, helping us to maintain our sanity. The whole staff worked in complete harmony and cooperation, even though each ward had, for two days, double its usual number of patients. The ward I was on had 160, but with many orderlies working and extra nurses on shift, we handled the workload.

The aftermath of the explosion was almost too pathetic and grim to describe. Only a few hours after dawn following the raid we began to realize that most of our patients had been contaminated by something beyond all imagination.

I first noticed it when one or two of my patients went to the sink looking for a drink of water. This was odd, because drinks had already been taken around as usual after supper. Suddenly there were more looking for water and we could hardly control them. They were complaining of intense heat and began stripping their clothes off. Patients confined to bed were trying desperately to rip their dressings and bandages off.

With what little knowledge we had, our first thought was that these boys were suffering from mustard gas burns. There were blisters as big as balloons and heavy with fluid on these young bodies. We were not sure whether the staff was at risk as we did not know what that fluid contained. Although we tried to get tests done, we were never informed of the results. We did everything humanly possible – draining the blisters, constant intravenous and eventually mild sedatives, but it was no good. It was horrible to see these boys, so young and in so much obvious pain. We couldn't even give them strong sedatives, since we weren't quite sure how they would react with whatever had poisoned them.

The medical officers tried to get through to the War Office in London for information, advice and an antidote, but none was forthcoming. We were all furious. And yet, if the war office couldn't release information, it must be a military secret, and if that was the case, we were certain we were witnessing the effects of a poison gas. Although we didn't know it at the time, there was indeed the very worst kind of poison gas involved.

Both day and night staff now were on duty. Despite our ministrations, we were at a loss to battle this poison and we couldn't save the majority of the wounded; almost 1000 men died in one night and just as many in the aftermath. I think they knew we were doing our best to save them. We tried to help make their last hours as painless as possible. Most of them were conscious throughout their ordeal and were so confused about their injuries. Their eyes asked us questions we couldn't answer.

Most of those dear boys probably lie buried somewhere in Bari. Some may not even have names, but they will never be forgotten by the Q.A.s who were with them as they slipped quietly away.

We felt so betrayed, and yet after it was all over we realized that had the incident been made public, the consequences may have been far worse. Who knew in those days what Germany was prepared to do?

I had always wanted confirmed what those men had been contaminated with, but my request to the British War Office even 30 years later produced no information. By sheer chance, through the Maritime Museum of the Atlantic in Halifax, Nova Scotia, I received information in April 1994 describing the Bari Raid.

It seems that a 50-year secrecy designation had expired and the magazine Shipping had noted the quietly released information. The following excerpts are taken from an article entitled "Mustard Gas Horror at Bari" written for the December 1993 edition of Shipping:

> ... On the afternoon of Dec. 2, 1943, the port was packed with ships unloading war supplies. The quays were a hive of activity, while other ships waited at various moorings for their turn to go alongside. There were more than 30 ships in the harbour, and most of those that were moored were concentrated

stern-to at the Nuova Molo Foranea, the outer mole known as the East Jetty.

Among the ships at the moorings was the Liberty cargo ship John Harvey ... owned by the U.S. War Shipping Administration and operated by Agwilines of New York. That late autumn, the ship had arrived at Baltimore where she took on a general cargo of ammunition and military stores – plus a special cargo of 2000, 100-pound mustard bombs ...

Late in the afternoon of December 2, a lone plane was spotted high in the sky over Bari. Many who saw it thought it was an Allied aircraft, for the Allies were said to dominate the skies over southern Italy. But the more experienced, particularly among the seamen, knew it to be a German reconnaissance plane. While the pilot of the German ME-210 aircraft could see the crowded harbour, what he could not have discovered was that the port was not that well defended – there were simply not enough antiaircraft weapons for a port of such importance and there was no fighter squadron on the city's airport tasked with defending the city. And most importantly, the radar installation that would give early warning of approaching aircraft was out of action ...

At 19:35, the first German Ju-88's arrived over Bari, achieving total surprise as they approached the harbour at about 150 feet. The first aircraft dropped flares to light up the harbour for the main bomber force. The first bombs soon fell on the city, damaging buildings and causing casualties among the servicemen and the locals but quickly the line of bombs crept towards the harbour.

In a matter of minutes, many ships were hit and set alight but it was among the ships moored at the East Jetty that the worst damage was done ...

Moments later there was another huge explosion. The John Harvey had blown up. The ship had broken loose from her moorings and began drifting across the harbour as the crew and the chemical experts on board tried to stop the flames reaching the cargo. The ship bore down on the tanker USS Pumper and just when it was feared the burning ship would inevitably hit the tanker, the John Harvey blew up. She disappeared completely. There were no survivors among those on board – the chemical specialists all died in this explosion. There was no one to warn the port authorities that the mustard was now seeping across the harbour in the cloud of smoke from the blast; there was just the odour of garlic – the odour of mustard gas – in the air …

The cloud of smoke from the explosion of the John Harvey carried the mustard over the harbour and then the town. Many Italians were killed when they fled from the city to escape the bombing and sought safety on the shore, only to die in the horror.

For the survivors of the ships, their real ordeal was only just beginning. It was worse for those who had been rescued from the water, covered in oil, for the oily slime covering the surface of the water had absorbed large quantities of the mustard. For many of these men, it might be several hours before their oil-soaked clothes would be removed, during which time the mustard had gone to work …

The German raid on Bari was a complete success [for the enemy]. Just two aircraft were lost while the Allies lost 17 ships carrying supplies. The attack set back the Allied campaign in Italy as well as depriving the Allies of a vital port, for it would be nearly a month before the port could be reopened. Most of the wrecks would be removed after the war in a major salvage operation that lasted many years …

A week or so later, after things had calmed down, I went back to check up on the patient for whom I had begun writing the letter. Someone else had finished it for him and sent it off. He didn't say so, but he must have been scared out of his wits hearing all the commotion without being able to see anything around him. Our medical officer almost decided to send him with the air evacuation, but he changed his mind for some reason and the patient stayed on with us after all. Those precious orderlies of ours looked after him and gave him many cups of tea when it was going around.

Ambulance Train to Ortona – January 1944

Despite the attempts of enemy aircraft and U-boats, the vast majority of the Allied ships entering the Mediterranean were now getting through safely. In June 1943 approximately 357 ships had passed through, and those numbers rose dramatically to an approximate total of 1012 in December. At the end of the year sailings of Mediterranean convoys actually exceeded those of Atlantic convoys. After the Bari Raid, the fighting kept moving up along the coast. As the army fought its way northwards toward the River Sangro, destroyers worked in support off both coasts of Italy and the Q.A.s followed in the ambulance trains.

I was next posted to an ambulance train known as the B-3, which made trips back and forth along the coast, picking up the wounded and bringing them back to the 98th General Base Hospital at Bari. I was accompanied by another Q.A. whom I believe was from Durham. The pair of us worked with two different crews who were both pleasant to work with and good company. The crew included an Indian cook who made certain that delectably spicy curries, rice and chapatis found their way to our table. The chapati looked something like an omelette but was very tough to chew. It was overwhelmingly popular with the Indians.

Our ambulance train initially wound its way along a route up the east coast of Italy between Bari and Ortona. As the army advanced, the train chugged up to Vasto, located just south of Ortona and a few miles beyond the famous Sangro River. Most of our patients at this time were from the city of Foggia, the biggest air base in south central Italy, around which the main battles were in progress. Quite often we transported patients – mostly New Zealand and Indian troops – south from Bari to Taranto for evacuation to the delta.

Once we returned to Bari from Taranto with a trainload of Italian POWs repatriated from North Africa. They didn't appear to be physically wounded, but they were extremely smelly and dirty and obviously worn out. We all breathed a collective sigh of relief when these patients were loaded off our train onto their native land, and we hoped that wherever they were going they could get a bath! Because of past experiences we had the train fumigated, just in case.

Our continual travels along the coast took us through the lovely, and at times snow-covered, countryside, with the magnificent Adriatic Sea always on one side. Once, our train was forced to crawl on newly laid track around a shelled railway tunnel; we were horrified to notice afterward the most awful sheer drop into the sea on the outer side. Although it appeared as if the train would fall over at any moment, we were apparently safe. The South African sappers on board were marvellous crewmen and knew the countryside and the abilities of the train; they were constantly reassuring us.

That we were an ambulance train seemed to make little difference to the enemy. One dusky afternoon as we were heading towards the front, a lone plane flew very low over our train and strafed us. There was nothing we could do about it. Fortunately the train was empty except for the staff, and it kept chugging along, its passengers praying that the train would not be hit too badly and that its drivers would remain unhurt. Our train was completely unarmed, with the large Red Cross painted on its side. The enemy plane flew off and the train came to a stop so the crew could examine the damage. They concluded that we had been lucky, coming away virtually unscathed.

Our experiences didn't always end well. On another occasion we were outside an area of fierce fighting waiting for a load of patients. We were sitting in a large field with trees on either side of us, waiting anxiously to get our patients and take them as fast as possible back to the base hospital. We were never sure by what mode of transportation the patients would come – by air or by road – so we weren't sure what to watch for. We suddenly spotted what was obviously a hospital plane flying low in the sky. It circled, coming toward us, seemingly alone. Almost before we knew it, the plane was on the ground completely engulfed in flames.

There was nothing we could do. We had been close enough to see the plane hit the ground and catch fire and we prayed that it was empty. But, sickeningly, we heard screams from the guts of the plane, above the roar of the flames. It was horrible. We stood together, a group of us, in the abutting field, watching while the twisted piece of metal burned well into the night. Sometime later we had it confirmed that the plane was indeed a hospital plane carrying the patients we had been waiting for.

About two weeks later, we were on our way to Ortona and about to cross the Sangro River when the train slowed to a halt and stopped for some time. After making inquiries we were told that the lines to the bridge crossing the river had been sabotaged – a switch had been thrown to divert trains from the brand-new Bailey bridge back to the old bridge which had been blown up.

The train travelling ahead of us had plunged into the river from the tracks that had led to the bombed-out bridge, and the engine driver had been pinned under water. They were amputating his leg in the water in order to save him.

The Bailey bridge had been designed by Donald Bailey, later Sir Donald Bailey, and it was described in a 1944 issue of Parade, the magazine of the Eighth Army:

> Mr. Donald Bailey of the Ministry of Supply, was travelling with a senior R.E. [Royal Engineering] officer to whom he outlined his ideas for a new type of equipment ... The officer was impressed and obtained permission for a trial "Bailey Bridge" to be constructed. It passed rigorous tests ... Bailey equipment consists of a set of interchangeable parts. The various sizes of bridges required are assembled by the piecing together of 10-foot sections; each section comprises seventeen parts and an additional nine for its foundation. Sections are linked together Meccano-like, one steel pin locking each joint securely. Sappers assemble the Bailey either on the remains of a demolished bridge or on pontoons. On land it is assembled on rollers and pushed across. If one span is not sufficient to bridge the gap, a second is rolled on top of the first, lowered into position and linked. The second and third ties are similarly pushed across. The longest Bailey Bridge is the 1200-foot structure spanning the Sangro River.

Our train was empty of patients and light and next in line, so we would be the first to use the Bailey bridge. The lost train's slide down the riverbank had weakened the ground under the near end of the new bridge, which stood close beside the old one, so there was room for doubt about the safety of the untested new bridge.

The Sangro is not a small river. We edged our way over it one foot at a time and it seemed to take forever. When we made it to the other end we sighed with relief while troops watching from both banks of the river cheered. When we returned a few days later, the bridge had been reinforced and was guarded.

We heard that the engine driver with the amputated leg had been taken to our hospital in Bari, so we visited him upon our return. He was weak and sick but thankful to be alive. We later heard, but had no chance to confirm, that he had been unable to keep up the struggle and had died in his sleep shortly after our visit.

Meeting Robert – February 1944

Our next trip to Ortona was February 8, 1944, memorable as it was my birthday but also because we had a new medical officer on board. Robert L. Aikens was a Canadian attached to the Royal Canadian Army Medical Corps who had come on staff at Bari from the Eighth Army. He was one of what they called the "borrowed" Canadians.

During the journey to Ortona we sat together and kept exchanging books of humorous writings. We found, to our surprise, that we had a similar sense of humour. The American and the British never seemed to see humour in the same way, and I had assumed Canadian humour was like the American. This Canadian, at least, seemed to appreciate the British sense of what could be funny.

We were extremely busy at the time and so, apart from having meals together in the staff car, I did not see very much of Robert until we returned to Bari. At that time, a few of us got together one evening and headed into town to see a local production of the Barber of Seville.

During our next trip up the Italian coast, Robert and I chatted about our respective parts of the world, sharing information about our respective families. Feeling rather domestic, and noting it appeared necessary, I also darned some of his socks for him as I couldn't imagine how he could be comfortable wearing socks with the toes out. I still do not know why there was yarn – white only – on the train; someone's idea of a medical supply?

I remember telling Robert, with great sympathy in my voice, how sorry I was to learn that he came from a country rarely free of snow and ice. He found that funny and we both ended up laughing about the image of poor Robert bundled up in a heavy parka, snow falling around him as he stepped gingerly across the ice! I remembered that I had an uncle living in Canada and told Robert that although my uncle's family had been trying for years to get him back to the U.K., where he could live a less rugged life, he simply refused to leave.

In the course of our travels, Robert and I became good friends. Knowing we might become separated at some point, we thought we would exchange photographs. We went into town one day to have them taken at one of the local shops. Mine looked awful, I thought, but we exchanged them anyway.

When there were no patients on the train a group of us worked together getting the approximately 300 stretchers ready for the next patients. We also had to arrange dressings and line up the drugs.

In order to keep up to date, we attended lectures by the medical officers. Robert came across as very intellectual and completely dedicated to his patients and his profession. He was extremely thorough.

One morning Robert delivered a detailed talk on sulpha drugs. He seemed nervous delivering his speech, and I sort of felt nervous for him. He was also talking about the new drug penicillin and stressing to us how terribly important it was. At that time, penicillin was treated like pure gold, so precious was it. Penicillin had been discovered and produced in the U.K. in 1940. Because of its scarcity and cost, a second, synthetic kind of penicillin was produced. It was much cheaper but equally effective and precious.

In the hospital in Bari, I saw how penicillin could save lives. One of my patients had been admitted with severe shrapnel wounds in his back. The wounds were horribly infected, reddish purple and filled with an ugly pus. This young man would surely have died without the administration of the wonder drug.

The patient sat up for the procedure known as insufflation, which was carried out with the utmost precision and frugality. A carefully measured amount of penicillin was brought in by the orderly in a special case. From a small teaspoon I would blow the penicillin into the wound through a special mask which protected the wounds from my germs and allowed precise aim. As I was cleaning the wound, I remember seeing the lung moving inside the chest wall. It was the first time I had ever witnessed something like that, and it was quite dramatic.

There was no romance between the doctor and me, but I felt very secure with him – until one day when my duties were in the same car of casualties as his and I suddenly became self-conscious. I could do nothing right; I dropped instruments, fell over things, got confused and flustered. It appeared to me that Robert was annoyed. We were extremely busy and I was his only assistant, so he was depending on me totally. I felt like such a fool and was so close to tears that I finally had to go into the next carriage and ask another nurse to exchange duties with me.

The following day I decided to find Robert and apologize for my frightful behaviour. A group of medical officers and nurses were heading into town, but I decided to stay behind and talk to Robert, However, I couldn't locate him.

When the group returned, I asked one of them about Robert and was told that Captain Aikens had been posted to Rome or somewhere near there and had left earlier that day. I was extremely upset and wished I could turn back the clock. "Why hadn't I gone to speak to Robert right away?" I asked myself. I had his picture framed and put it in my room, but I believed I would never see him again.

Our Major, a friend of mine and of Robert's and the head of the officers on the train, took me aside the next evening in the dining car. He told me that he knew Robert was very fond of me. He and Robert had become good friends and the Major told me that Robert was one of the nicest people and one of the best medical officers he'd ever met. The Major had Robert's address and suggested that I write to him. Apparently Robert had been posted to the 132nd Field Ambulance in Piccili about 15 miles south of Monte Cassino, another scene of long and fierce fighting.

Though Robert had spent a relatively short time aboard the ambulance train, we all missed him, I more than the rest. Quite often a group of us had gathered after dinner to listen to the letters Robert received from his home in Stellarton, Nova Scotia. Those letters were mostly from his mother, who relayed tidbits of information about Robert's two brothers, about his dad's work in his drugstore, Aikens Drugs, and about the goings-on in the community.

One day when we got back to Bari from one of our travels up the coast there had been a box of Nova Scotia russet apples waiting for Robert, a special treat from his mother. What a feast we had enjoyed as the apples made their way around. Even in wartime, despite all the fighting, the mail came through, keeping all of us in touch with our homes and families.

Four of us had made a wonderful team. Robert, the Major, a Q.A. named Elsie and I had similar interests and personalities. Our travels up and down the coast involved long, work-filled days and, after we had seen the patients safely onto the ambulances conveying them from our train to the hospital, we took a welcome respite. We would collect our mail, enjoy a long, hot bath or shower, pick out a fresh change of clothing and head downtown for a restaurant meal and often a show.

After a short time in Bari, it was back to the train. On the train, there were always one doctor, one nurse and orderlies on duty with the patients. When the train was full, everyone was on duty continuously, day and night, until we arrived back at Bari.

Most of the cars on the train were set up to accommodate the patients, with stretchers in two tiers occupying every available space. The staff were housed in a central carriage, with two officers occupying one tiny compartment and the Q.A.s in another. Between these two was a larger compartment which was used for reading, discussing patients' medical conditions, doing charts or playing records. We worked at a long table down the centre. Probably the most popular feature of the staffroom was the record player, on which could often be heard the tunes of Vera Lynn.

On one of our trips into the city, we purchased a recording of the Barber of Seville, as we had enjoyed the opera so much. Each time we put the record on after that, Robert would get out the mandolin he had purchased locally and strum along to the music. He soon got very good.

Storytelling was also a favourite pastime. One evening, after the patients had all been comfortably settled and some of us were relaxing in the staff car, Robert told us about the driver who had been with him in the desert. All officers had batmen and we had a marvellous one on the train, a Cockney who looked after the needs of the four of us. According to dictionary definition, a batman is "a military servant." Robert's batman had been the designated driver of a jeep which was returning to the camp one day after picking up supplies. He drove over a mine and the jeep and driver were blown up. Because Robert had been good friends with the batman, his death had upset him terribly. Later, when in England, he tried to locate the batman's family.

That same evening, after the story of the batman, Robert related a more humorous incident. He had arrived in Egypt and had set up his belongings in his tent and was then called to make a trip out for some reason or another. As he drove out across the desert with another chap, in the middle of nowhere there appeared a large sign and then another and another: "No Tipping" in bold letters. Robert explained to us how he had looked around, but for the life of him couldn't see any restaurants or canteens or waiters standing about expectantly. He finally had to ask one of the officers what the signs meant. We all burst out laughing when Robert told us that the signs meant that rubbish could not be dumped there!

Captain Aikens had told me all sorts of things about his family and the route he had taken to get to where he now was. Robert had been born in the town of Stellarton in the province of Nova Scotia, Canada. His father was a pharmacist with his own drugstore in the heart of the town; his mother a housewife raising three boys, of which Robert was the middle child.

Robert's father had lost a lot of money in the Depression and it was a struggle to live as well as they had before. However, Robert was determined to continue his studies after graduating with a gold medal at Pictou Academy in Stellarton. He had graduated from Dalhousie University in Halifax with his medical degree in 1939 and had interned at a large hospital in Montreal.

He had volunteered for war service with the British army and sailed for England with the Royal Canadian Army Medical Corps on loan to the British forces. He had been all over North Africa and involved in many key battles before joining us at Bari.

Robert had been stationed in Tripoli in June 1943 when King George VI visited the Fourth Indian Division on an inspection tour of the troops and hospitals. The King was accompanied by General Montgomery, whose victories at Alamein and Tobruk had made him a hero. Robert had been in both of those campaigns.

King George VI and General Montgomery visiting troops in North Africa. Above, the King stands in the Jeep, the General is seated, wearing a beret. Below, the King inspects the troops, General Montgomery stands with another officer.

Robert in a tent in North Africa

Montgomery had spread the idea that the Eighth Army was an independent striking force, taking its orders from no one. Not only was he a brilliant strategist with a very solid military training, he was also one of the boys and got along well with his troops. Robert held a keen admiration and respect for him.

Almost immediately after Robert's departure, the ambulance train was ordered south to Taranto to deliver a group of patients to a hospital ship that would take them to the U.K. The Major was about to be transferred, and we left Bari in such haste that there was no time to get his address. We were driven back to Bari by ambulance, and the Major had departed before we arrived. I keenly regretted losing touch with him.

He was married to a Frenchwoman and they had settled in the south of England to raise their three children. Such a wonderful person, he had kept reassuring me that Robert and I would get back together and reminded me a last time to write to Captain Aikens. I know he would have been delighted to hear how Robert and I turned out.

I did finally send off a letter to Robert, somewhat tentatively, wondering if I would get a reply; Robert answered right away. We wrote to each other regularly and so began what turned out to be a romance through letters. It was amazing how quickly the letters got through in both directions, especially with all the fighting going on at Robert's posting in Monte Cassino.

The battle there centred on an ancient Benedictine monastery perched on the top of a high cliff. The Germans were using it as a fortress and they could see every move below. On March 12, almost every type of combat plane that could be assembled had bombed the German stronghold and the British troops had captured the position.

After dozens of letters exchanging pleasantries only, due to the extreme secrecy, a letter came one day in which Robert asked if I would join him on his off-duty leave. He seemed to know that hospital staff were being given leave and spending it at a place near Naples. As he was due for leave, he wanted to know if I could also get some scheduled time off so that we could see each other. The British hospital staff were permitted to take a few days leave when things were relatively quiet and predesignated locations had been chosen for that purpose. I inquired and found out that we Q.A.s were permitted to spend four days at a Young Womens Christian Association (YWCA) in Sorrento, Italy.

Sorrento – July 1944

I had to make my own arrangements for transportation to Sorrento, but as vehicles were constantly driving north carrying medical equipment and replacements, the nursing Sisters could usually hitch a ride with them. I asked around and learned that a truck was driving out the next afternoon and at 2:00 p.m. the next day the truck left with me on it. Unfortunately, it went only as far as an airfield, about halfway, so I hopped into the ambulance plane which was on a brief stopover at the airfield and flew into Naples. From there, I was escorted on the back of a dispatch rider's motorcycle for a short run to another Red Cross ambulance and from there it was straight on to Sorrento.

I had packed only a tiny bag with nightclothes, mufti, an extra sweater and toiletries, but I was happy to see that I still had it with me in Sorrento after all that switching around! I had long ago decided, after losing my trunk with all its precious belongings on the Strathallan, that I would always travel light.

I arrived at the YWCA in Sorrento, feeling a little bit tired and jostled by my excursion. I had certainly experienced every available mode of transportation in this war! I headed for the bath, sent my uniform out to the laundry and got into civilian garb. It felt wonderful to be in comfortable, non-uniform clothing. A couple of hours later, Robert met me downstairs and took me to a lovely little cafe where we had a delightfully romantic dinner. Seeing him again, I realized just how much I had missed him.

After dinner we sat on the cafe's balcony and talked of many things, one of which was the day on the ambulance train when I had been so nervous. Robert didn't recall my being clumsy or dropping things and certainly didn't think he had been irritated. He said he had probably been focussed on the job at hand and wouldn't have been thinking about anything else. I was happy to hear that. From the street below us came the muted sounds of people passing; the war seemed far away at that moment.

Robert and I said our goodnights before the Y's 11:00 p.m. curfew, and I made sure he signed the book before leaving. Our activities were carefully scrutinized at the Y; I had to sign in and out just like the guests.

The building was like a convent, deathly quiet, and our footsteps seemed to echo loudly. In hindsight, I suppose the atmosphere was merely restful and that we had almost forgotten what peace and quiet was like. Robert was staying at a tiny inn nearby. We set a time to meet the following morning, and I waved after him as he walked off.

I was used to the early mornings and rose easily at 6:00, dressed and sat on the Y's balcony enjoying the scenery until Robert called for me. He was used to rising early as well. We would stroll around the streets down by the water, window-shopping and enjoying the morning sunshine and fresh air before choosing a little spot for breakfast.

We visited San Michele, Amalfi and a Byzantine cathedral, and on one afternoon we took a boat tour to the Isle of Capri. Capri had been commandeered by the United States, so it was easy to get back and forth on day excursions. Our tour guide pointed out many sights, one of which was the home of Gracie Fields, the English singer who had married an Italian and was almost exiled by the British because of it. Their estate in Capri was palatial.

We discovered on the boat tour that both of us were terrible sailors, but because the scenery was so breathtaking we decided we should focus our attention on that and forget our maladies. Easier said than done.

One of the sights we both wanted to see was the Blue Grotto. As we boarded the boat, looking around us for signs of other passengers, we realized that we would be the only two people going on a boat that could have held at least twenty. The skipper was an Italian, one of Britain's former enemies, and he didn't look the least bit friendly. I was somewhat nervous; judging by the expression on Robert's face, I think even he was a bit apprehensive.

When we had slipped far into the depths of the cave they called the Blue Grotto, the water became so crystal clear that we could easily see the bottom. It was a long, long way down and my overactive imagination suddenly conjured up pictures of the skipper dumping us both overboard. "If we disappeared we probably wouldn't be missed," I thought, "not for a while anyway … even if someone did notice us missing, where would they think to look for us?" These thoughts did nothing to add to the enjoyment of our little voyage, and I watched anxiously until we finally emerged from the cave and sailed back to the dock.

We returned to the YWCA and once again relaxed on the balcony, sipping strong, hot coffee. Robert started pointing to the stars and naming the different constellations and planets. I told him that I did not know one star from another and he took me totally by surprise when he said, "Marry me and I'll teach you all about them."

After catching my breath, I replied that I couldn't because I had promised my mother that I would be married only in Wales. What that had to do with marrying Robert I am not really sure. As an equally brilliant afterthought, I explained that I couldn't possibly live in Canada with all that ice and snow. Robert just said, "Let's go into Naples tomorrow and get a ring."

We really did make the trip into Naples the following day. Robert and I visited a little jewellery shop and we spent about an hour looking at rings. Together we picked out a very pretty ring, an aquamarine surrounded by tiny diamonds which seemed to have been made just for my finger. I put it on, we both liked it, Robert paid for it and that was it! We came out of the store slightly confused, I think. I turned my hand this way and that, and Robert said, "There! You're engaged to me now and we can get married in Wales." To him, it seemed logical and simple.

I wondered if we might be rushing things a bit, and I asked Robert if he was sure we were doing the right thing and if perhaps we shouldn't think a little more about this. He replied that he'd been thinking of nothing else since we last left the train in Bari. "You'll just have to put up with all that ice and snow, I guess." The rest of that afternoon we strolled the streets, arm in arm, and every so often Robert would look at me and my left hand, as if just to make sure the ring was still in place.

I didn't want that day to end, but it was getting late and we had to get back to Sorrento. We said goodbye at YWCA door and agreed to meet again in the morning to take in a few more sights before my return to Bari. It had been quite a day and we were both very tired, although pleasantly so.

Robert had arranged everything for my departure by plane tomorrow, so there was nothing more for me to do that night except pack my little bag, have a good sleep and dream a future in the land of ice and snow. Robert and I had no idea that Sorrento and Capri were romantic – to us they were permitted and convenient places in which to get away from the horrible war.

Return to Bari

It seemed strange being back on duty after those four glorious and eventful days in Sorrento. In that short period a number of my friends had been posted to other areas and it was lonely at first without them around. But with so many patients to look after, there was little time for feeling lonely.

Like the patient I had nursed in Tunis, one of my patients here in Bari also kept busy writing poetry while he convalesced. He wrote one piece which he called Bella Italia which I thought was so good that I tucked it away for safekeeping. Much later, after hearing that this young fellow had been killed while returning to his home in England, I found the poem and read it over to myself once again.

BELLA ITALIA

If I was an artist with nothing to do,
I'd paint a picture, a composite view
Of historic Italy in which I'd show
Visions of contrast, high and low.

Castle and palace and opera house too,
Hotel, town and mountain, a marvellous view,
Homes made of wood, bricks and mud,
People covered with scabs, scurvy and blood.

Chapels and churches, great to behold,
Each a king's ransom, glittering gold.
Poverty and want, men craving for food,
Picking through garbage, practically nude.

Stately cathedrals with huge-toned bells,
Ricovero shelters with horrible smells,
Moulding catacombs, a place for the dead,
Noisy civilians, clamouring for bread.

Palatial villas with palm trees tall,
A stinking hovel, near hole in the wall.
Tree-fringed lawns, swept by the breeze,
Goats wading in filth up to their knees.

Revealing statues, all details complete,
A sensual lass, with souls on her feet,
Creeping boulevards, a spangled team,
Alleys that wind like a dope fiend's dream.

A sidewalk latrine with privacy nil,
Flowers blooming on the side of a hill,
Two-by-four shops with shelves all bare,
Gesturing merchants, arms flailing the air.

Narrow-gauge sidewalk, more like a shelf,
Butt-puffing youngster scratching himself,
Lumbering carts hogging the road,
Nondescript trucks frequently towed.

Diminutive donkey, less than its load,
Its owner treating it not as he should.
Elegant caskets carved out of wood,
Odorous wine shops where vino is brewed.

A shoemaker's shop, a black-market store,
Crawling with vermin and beetles galore.
I've tried to describe the things I have seen,
Panorama of Italy, the brown and the green.

I've neglected the war scars, visible yet,
But these are the things we want to forget.
I'm not glad that I came to find it so,
Give it back to the natives, I'm ready to go.

Booklet handmade by the author of "Bella Italia"

It was a few months before I heard again from Robert. He was now in Rome for a short period. The battle was moving north, and as we were getting busier, I thought that it was likely just as bad where Robert was. Fighting was also intense in Yugoslavia and Greece, and many casualties arriving in the Bari hospital were from these countries.

At this time, the army called for volunteers for parachute training. The plan was to parachute medical teams into Yugoslavia in order to help with the enormous numbers of wounded. I knew that I could never drop out of an airplane – the very thought made me shudder. Some were willing to go and others, like myself, who simply couldn't bring themselves to it no matter how much they wanted to assist their country!

Once again there was not enough room for everyone in the hospital building, so many of our patients were cared for in large tents.

Although the British army did not have women troops, other countries did, and many of our patients coming in from countries like Greece and Yugoslavia were female. It was a rather strange sight, all these uniformed women. But then, I suppose we Q.A.s had looked just as peculiar in our battledress! These female soldiers were badly wounded and very dirty and had to be deloused before treatment could be administered.

One night, a female Yugoslav soldier arrived who was very pregnant. Not only that, but our Colonel provided a private room for her, which was far out of the ordinary. Another Q.A. on duty and I were given explicit instructions by the Colonel: if the woman went into labour in the night, he wanted to be contacted immediately and he was adamant that the other Q.A. and I, both of us state certified midwives trained in England, would be there with her in case of difficulties.

Doctors and obstetricians were supposed to be on hand for any abnormal or emergency deliveries which might occur. But here, of course, things were different and I hoped that everything would go smoothly.

Some hours after we had received the Colonel's instructions, the woman went into labour and I confidently delivered the baby to the weary mother. I think she had expected the Colonel to be there, but he had been unable to get back from wherever he had gone, despite our notification to him.

Those like myself who were curious discovered later that this woman was the wife of one of the Yugoslav resistance leaders. I often wondered whose son I had delivered, but everything was so strictly confidential that I never did find out.

Emergency in Wales

I received some disturbing news from home. My mother was seriously ill in hospital. I applied for compassionate posting to the U.K. My mother was so unselfish that she would never have thought of sending for me, but I knew that after a very serious and difficult operation for the removal of a kidney, she would be happy to see her only child.

I wrote to Robert explaining it all to him, but didn't receive a reply before I left for home. That was not surprising, as I had heard that the fighting was still pretty grim around Monte Cassino.

The arrangements were made quickly, and I left the hospital for the docks at Naples and the boat which would carry me back to Wales. I suppose I must have been daydreaming while waiting on the dock for the boat, because I felt a sharp tug at my elbow and realized in horror that a thief had just stolen my handbag by cutting the shoulder strap.

I was both furious and close to tears. Not only had my passport been in that bag, but more importantly to me, my mother's engagement ring, which she had given to me for good luck as I left the U.K. for active service. I used to wear it on a chain around my neck, but I had put the ring in my bag, perhaps for safekeeping. While off duty I was wearing Robert's ring, but why I hadn't put my mother's ring on another finger I will never know.

I was more upset about the ring than about the passport until it struck me that the loss of a military passport was a serious military offence. The passport could have been picked up and used by the enemy and I could be court-martialled! Naples, this idyllic spot of my engagement to Robert, now looked bleak.

There was no time to have a passport reissued as I was supposed to be boarding the ship soon and it certainly wouldn't wait for me. So, I was escorted to the Colonel's office on the docks, where I met with the Colonel and went over the unfortunate purse-snatching incident with him. I then related my story all over again before a hastily assembled Court of Inquiry and was finally issued a temporary passport. I suppose I deserved all the reprimanding I received from the Colonel and the military court, but that thought didn't make me any happier.

With thoughts of Mother and thoughts of Robert on my mind, I felt so unhappy and alone that it seemed as if my whole world was falling in around me. I stayed on deck most of the time, gulping in the fresh sea air and nibbling on hard, dry rolls to calm my queasy stomach. It was a long, miserable and uneventful journey back to the U.K. on what I believe was one of the Empress boats. But the weather cooperated and the journey, though not pleasant, was a vast improvement over the rocky voyage in the Strathallan. I spent as much time as I could outside, either reading or walking around, and retired to my cabin early in the evening.

One fellow passenger was a naval officer who sat beside me one day and struck up a friendly conversation. When he found out where I was headed, he said that he didn't live very far away and offered me a drive to the train station when we got into Liverpool. His wife was coming to meet him and they would be happy to give me a lift. We disembarked at Liverpool and his wife was at the bottom of the ramp waiting to give him a big hug. As soon as the bags were packed away in the trunk of the car, off we drove to the train station.

To my embarrassment, we found out that the next train to Wales was not leaving until early tomorrow morning. Just as I was beginning to feel desperation set in again, these wonderful people suggested that I go back to their home for the night. I could have cried – tears of joy this time – and I didn't hesitate in taking them up on their offer.

Close by they were, as it took no more than five minutes to drive to their home, a tiny stone bungalow on a quiet street. The instant we walked through the door, two small children were shouting with delight at seeing their father again and the household came alive with noisy, happy conversation.

Although I hadn't thought I was hungry, I had no difficulty eating everything put before me at dinner. Later I was shown to the bed in the children's room, which I politely refused, opting instead for the living room sofa. I would have been able to sleep anywhere.As the sun's rays poked through the curtains the next morning, I felt refreshed and much happier. I got a drive into the station and boarded the train after saying my goodbyes. Chugging away from the city, looking out at the dreary urban landscape flitting by, I remember thinking, for some reason, that I had never seen so many smoking chimneys in my life.

It was only long after the train had pulled away from the station that I realized that I hadn't even got the name or address of the wonderful couple who had taken me into their home. I shook my head in disbelief and made a mental note to try and get in touch with them if I could. They would never know how very grateful I was to them.

U.K.

1945

Home Again in Wales – January 1945

The train wended its way to the little station in north Wales, and as I alighted, once again that feeling of despair welled up in me. There was no one in sight to greet me. I sat patiently, waiting for my luggage to be unloaded off the train, but it seemed to have disappeared and no one seemed to know anything about it or to care. It was bitterly cold, the nip of a wind taunting me as I stood shivering and feeling absolutely miserable and alone. The station seemed to be little more than a dropping-off spot for a few passengers; there were no taxis in sight and not even a phone booth from which to call one. This was, after all, wartime Britain and everyone seemed to be away.

I finally tracked down the stationmaster and explained to him quite abruptly that I had just returned from overseas. He said expressionlessly that I must be happy to be back. I replied that I wasn't happy at all – I had lost my luggage and wasn't sure how I was going to get to my house. I asked him where all the taxis were and he sort of looked at me blankly and said that I could phone for one inside, if I wanted to. He wasn't treating me with the respect or recognition I thought I deserved, having just come over from the scene of the war. He was reserved and aloof. I was indignant. And then he told me.

He had lived in London all his life. A few weeks ago his house had been blown to pieces in a single bomb blast. He had lost his home, his wife and his three precious children all in one night. He was still alive because he had been on duty that night as an air-raid warden.

His brother in North Wales had offered him a home and had also secured him the job with the railway. The previous stationmaster had been called up and sent to Europe with the invasion troops and no one knew when or if he would return.

I suddenly felt terribly selfish and wished with all my heart that there was something I could do for him. I just stood there looking at him, silently acknowledging the bitter realities of war. He shrugged his shoulders and looked away for a moment. I followed him into the station house, where I found my luggage waiting and he called me a cab.

The home situation I was returning to didn't please me at all. My grandmother had taken ill with a stroke not long ago and there was no one else but my mother to look after her. She was not unwilling, but she was still recovering from her kidney operation, and she should have been resting and nurturing her own fragile health. This was not Swansea, where she had raised me, but north Wales, to which she had moved to get away from the war, with no telephone, car or central heating.

However, upon my arrival her usual good spirits burst forth. She was surprised and overjoyed to see me and it was wonderful to be with her again. I think she thought that because I was home it meant that the war was coming to an end and everyone was now returning home. I couldn't tell her that this wasn't the case.

I didn't want to tell my mother that I had requested a compassionate posting just to be with her. She wouldn't have wanted me to interrupt my duties. But I wouldn't have done anything else. The look on my mother's face when I gave the news of my impending marriage made it all worthwhile. Mother was eager to meet this Canadian officer who had "stolen her daughter's heart."

The British army did not allow its medical or nursing personnel to leave the service just because a family member was in ill health. Instead they posted the individual to a hospital close to the place they would be visiting while on leave.

After helping at home, conferring with Mother's doctor and arranging for more domestic help, I felt that her situation was reasonably stable. I left for my next posting to a hospital in mid-Wales about an hour away from my mother's home. Waiting for the train, I looked around for the stationmaster, but he wasn't there. I wanted so much to apologise.

There were few passengers on the train and it was damp and cold. As the train meandered through the wilds of Wales, my window became streaked with tiny droplets. The fields boasted clusters of daffodils, all bowing their heads in the gentle rain. In late January, it wasn't uncommon to see the fields crowded with flowers, and the touch of colour they added in the mist was refreshing.

Buckland House, Wales

One funny thing about this trip was the name of the stops I had to make. I had to change in Builth to get to Bwlch. Difficult to say when you're shivering as I was! I am Welsh, but not a Welsh speaker.

At the Bwlch station, I was met by an army truck and uniformed driver and taken to the most gorgeous estate I had ever seen. Masses of brilliant daffodils flanked the structure, an imposing mansion surrounded by a sea of vibrant colours. I thought the house looked just like the one in Daphne DuMaurier's book, *Rebecca.*

We had arrived at Buckland House, one of the many private mansions which had been converted for war purposes. The house was now a military hospital of about 1000 patients. It ministered both to men wounded in home base exercises and to men from the base hospitals overseas who would convalesce from permanent injuries here.

Although I wouldn't be staying inside the main house, curiosity demanded a quick look around. The house was a multistorey stone construction with a multitude of windows ushering in a flood of light. The hallways were spacious and the rooms simply decorated.

I ventured outside again, walking around to the rear of the structure. The grounds probably covered 60 acres or more, and everywhere were elegantly manicured flowerbeds and close-cropped shrubbery. A narrow cobbled pathway led from the house and down to the pretty river Usk. Its banks were edged with proud stands of hardwood and lush evergreens, and everywhere were scattered tiny wildflowers.

It would have been marvellous to stay in the main house, but the Q.A.s posted here lived in nissen huts, which were temporary buildings shaped like tunnels and constructed of corrugated iron with doors at both ends. They were named after Peter Nissen, a British engineer, and were meant to provide quick, safe housing for large groups of people or equipment. There had been quite a few of the distinctive huts around when I left for overseas in 1942, and by my return in 1945 they had proliferated.

As I entered the hut assigned to me, I noticed immediately the mousetraps placed in strategic locations on the cement floor. "Great," I thought, "if it's not bedbugs, it's mice!" Apart from the traps, whoever I was sharing the hut with had made the place quite comfortable and lived-in.

As I glanced around I spotted one of those familiar black metal regulation-size trunks supporting a number of hard-covered books between two large bookends. The name painted in bold white lettering on the side of the trunk – HARVEY – wasn't familiar, but that little black trunk certainly brought back memories. So much had happened since I had seen my own black trunk loaded on the Strathallan; it seemed as though years had gone by. After unpacking and changing into something more comfortable, I decided to see who else was around.

I hurried through a light drizzle across the damp lawns of the estate to another nissen hut which was used as a dining and relaxation centre for the nursing Sisters. On the grey cement floor sat three or four tin buckets, full of rainwater which had leaked in during the morning's heavy rain. With a lonely plop, plop, plop, water still dripped from a hole in the roof. A heavy old burlap curtain divided the interior into dining area and sitting room. Commanding the living room was a huge, wide coke stove whose intense heat was welcome. Next to the stove stood a large metal receptacle filled with old papers, scraps of wood and anything else which would fuel the fire. Someone had thoughtfully placed tiny pots of fresh flowers here and there to add a bit of colour.

A few Q.A.s sat in hard wood chairs, their fingers nimbly flying with wool and needles. On one lap a sweater was taking shape almost before my eyes. I introduced myself and took up a position in one of the chairs. Finally I was drawn into conversation, and gradually we began chatting about everything from sweaters to war. A weather-beaten radio crackled with the voice of a news announcer in the Far East and one of the girls told us that she had just returned from four years in India.

We moved into the other room for supper, still carrying on our different conversations. I retired to my hut shortly after the meal, deciding to get to bed early. My roommate was away that night and I fell asleep quickly.

It didn't seem long before I was awakened by a scratching sound and the unmistakable crackle of paper. I found my flashlight on the nightstand and shone it around the room. On the ledge above the desk across the room a mouse was cheekily nibbling the corner of a chocolate bar, wrapper and all. He had ignored the cheese in the mouse-trap and seemed quite unconcerned by me and my light.

I threw a shoe at the ledge, just missing the little rascal, who scampered away. I crawled back into my bed, pulling the covers tightly up to my chin and peering out over my toes for any sign of the creature.

I awoke the next morning with the blankets still pulled close around me and felt rather silly. At a sound close by I looked around and found my roommate. She had arrived early that morning and, not wanting to wake me, had been quietly reading a book. Something made me look again. My roommate was none other than Nora Wells, my friend from Peebles! After astonished exclamations and hugs, we fell to talking, laughing and reminiscing.

Nora had married her medical officer, which of course accounted for the surname Harvey on the trunk. She and her husband lived in the tiny town of Monmouth, not far away from Buckland House, and had been fortunate to move into the large house which had belonged to her husband's parents. As a married nurse, Nora could have a home posting to the U.K. Her husband was in a unit not too far away.

It was because of the home posting that Nora had been missing from the Strathallan group leaving Peebles. She had been unaware that the group I was in had left for overseas, nor had she heard of our shipwreck, which came as quite a shock. After reliving for her some of the details of the sinking and the storybook rescue, I happily informed her of my engagement to Robert.

Nora suggested that we could all get together in Monmouth on Robert's return and I told her I would mention this in my next letter to him, which I did that very evening. Robert expressed delight that Nora and I had become reunited. He said that everyone thought the war would soon be over, and as troops were slowly returning home, it shouldn't be too much longer. I think he was happy I was safely waiting for him in the U.K.

Soon I received another letter from Robert informing me that he had been posted back to the Middle East. In a way I was pleased because conditions in the north of Italy, where he had been from the end of February 1944, were not very good. We had hoped that any further postings would have been to the U.K., but I suppose that was too much to ask.

G. Aikens on a footbridge over the River Usk, 1945. The Q.A. non-duty uniform jacket had evolved to resemble the men's uniforms the Q.A.s wore in Algiers after the 1942 sinking of the Strathallan.

The Buckland hospital unit was very orderly and structured. The patients stayed on here longer and the numbers remained fairly constant – we weren't likely to have 30 patients one day and suddenly 60 or 70 the next. Nor were we likely to work 20 hours one day and then be off for the next two days as had been the case in the war-zone hospitals. Our on-duty time would be similar to the civilian hospitals' – 8:00 a.m. to 8:00 p.m., half an hour for meals and then an extra hour or two off at a certain part of the day.

Night duty was the same, and we were required to sleep a certain number of hours during the day. Buckland was so wonderfully quiet that it was a joy to crawl into my little bed and sleep peacefully for six hours or so with no bombs, gunfire or planes to disturb me. Although we were kept on our feet at Buckland House, it was in no way comparable to the gruelling routine we had endured in our nursing duties overseas.

We cared for wounded soldiers, but there were other types of injuries too. One day a patient was brought in from field exercises on the range where the troops had been target shooting with antiaircraft. Somehow, an explosion close by this young man had thrown him into the air, hurling him across the field with tremendous force. He was rushed in for surgery, his friends still shocked at this turn of events.

But I was even more shocked when he was just about ready for the surgical procedure. The doctor suddenly extinguished all the lights in the operating theatre and the patient almost lit up the room, giving off an eerie green phosphorescent glow. I had never seen anything like it. This patient was so badly burned with phosphorous that he had to be kept heavily sedated and we had to keep all his dressings cold and wet.

Something which I found fascinating and somewhat amusing was the politics of two of our house guests at Buckland House. Politics had never really entered my life and communism was a word that rarely if ever crossed my lips. My family had voted the same way for as long as I could remember, and although never strongly politically motivated, had always supported the traditional parties. An acquaintance of my mother who worked in Russia and returned home with communist tendencies was more or less socially exiled.

I got my introduction into the communist way of thinking from these two men, obvious communist sympathizers, whom I got to know fairly well. They were from extreme ends of the social ladder. One was an orderly who had taught at length on the politics of communism. The other was an aristocrat, an officer who was, if I recall correctly, the grandson of a lord, born with the proverbial silver spoon in his mouth. Neither man openly confessed to being a communist but it was obvious. The conversations of the two of them made for some colourful dialogue.

The Colonel in charge at Buckland House was a nice chap, with an endearing charm and charisma. He often surprised us just before dinnertime with a succulent, fresh salmon caught, we suspected, very quietly in the river Usk. We didn't say anything to anyone.

The Colonel could also be seen in his off-duty hours splitting logs for our fires, the main source of our heat. He would toss the split logs into a large woodpile and then stack his arms full and bring them into our main nissen hut. I think he rather enjoyed the exercise, as he always had a smile on his face despite the sweat on his brow.

Unfortunately, although the river was beautiful and produced lovely salmon, it also attracted mice and rats. Not only did we have to contend with these creatures in our residences, as my experience with the mouse had shown, but we also had to put up with them in the wards. One morning, just after I had come on duty and was beginning the round of dressings, I was sickened by a horrible sight.

One of our patients, injured by small-arms fire during exercises at the range, was recovering from an operation on his jaw. He had been heavily sedated because of the pain and had been sleeping most of the time. When I approached his bedside to change his dressing, I found to my horror that the dressing had been partially torn away and was hanging in shreds from his face. The only plausible conclusion was that a rat had eaten it away in the night. Fortunately the wound had been closed by metal clips or there is no telling what might have happened. It simply was not possible to put a guard at the bottom of each bed and our anti-rodent precautions were not perfectly effective. I shuddered to think how the soldier would have felt had he awakened to find a rat by his face.

About a month into my stay at Buckland, Victory in Europe Day, or VE Day, signalling the end of the war in Europe, was proclaimed. A sense of joy, peace and happiness abounded. I was ecstatic because I could now look forward to marrying Robert upon his arrival in the U.K. The day warranted a celebration of life, and so Nora and I and a few others put on our walking shoes and headed off to the adjoining fields.

We watched the labourers tending to their crops and livestock and we leaned against the fences, captivated by the antics of the lambs. The countryside was ablaze with the rosy hues of the rhododendrons, which seemed to stretch on forever along the roadways. The Breckon Beacons, a range of mountains running through the centre of south Wales, were faintly outlined off in the distance, their sun-sparkling peaks stretching skyward.

The friendship which had begun in Peebles between Nora and me flourished at Buckland. Because she had been on staff at the house for so long and because she could get home frequently, she was able to provide numerous comforts. One was an amazing invention called, I think, Teasmade, which was an automatic electrical contraption for making tea. Just before we retired, one of us would put water into the kettle and tea in the pot and then switch the machine to the automatic setting.

At 6:00 the following morning the alarm would go off, the radio would turn on, the water would be boiling and presto, the tea was made. We had set up our wonder machine on the table between our two beds, so when the tea was made we sat up, poured, and lay back in bed luxuriously, listening to the news. We sometimes listened to a "On Your Toes," an exercise program. We would drink our tea, and then get up and do our stretching and bending in time with the exercise announcer and the peppy music. The combination of tea and exercises got us warmed up quite quickly through the short but chilly winter.

Vera Lynn's voice could be heard everywhere, it seemed. Songs like "Yours Till the End of Life's Story'" and "You'll Never Know How Much I Love You" were played over and over again, their lyrics forming on our lips automatically. These were the songs that the war had produced, songs that made us quickly blink our eyes, trying not to let our emotions take hold, as we remembered friends we had worked alongside but never heard from again, cities weary of bombing and destruction and the soldiers we had tried to keep from death's door.

When I heard Vera Lynn's voice I saw Robert merrily strumming along on his mandolin in the dining compartment of our ambulance train. Songs from the Barber of Seville reminded me, again, of Robert, lips set in a serious line and eyebrows arched, pretending to conduct the overture. What a ham he could be! And how I missed him.

Buckland House seemed to be a hive of information, perhaps because there were more compassionate and home postings going through here from overseas. One evening I recounted a story a young guard had told me. One day his Colonel came through, showed an identity card. The guard saluted and the Colonel walked off. The Colonel then returned to the guard post and showed the guard his card again. "Now look at that carefully and tell me if that looks anything like me." Of course it was someone else's card with a different photograph, and it must have been embarrassing for the young chap, who had not wanted to challenge a higher-ranking officer but who did indeed get punished for his lax behaviour. They all had to be so careful.

Some other news was more disturbing. One of my Q.A. friends from Peebles who had been on the Strathallan and worked with us in Algiers, a well educated girl and dedicated nurse, had become pregnant and was dismissed from the army and sent home.

The officer involved had admitted his responsibility, but he had a wife in the U.K. Whether he had been cashiered, the teller didn't know. This would have meant loss of rank and any pay due. By admitting that he was the father he might have won a lesser sentence.

An unmarried Q.A. who became pregnant in wartime was sent home in disgrace from the army and would not be allowed to work in a civilian hospital. Her name would be struck off the roll of midwives and she would probably be taken off the Royal College of Nurses register. This young girl's future would be very bleak. I remembered her telling us about falling in love with some chap while in Algiers, but I didn't think too much about it at the time.

Summer arrived, and June was a beautiful month in Wales. The birds chirruped constantly, the countryside was ablaze with colour and we could enjoy it, as work had slowed down considerably.

One warm summer morning, I stopped for coffee in the duty room – we never went away from the wards, but took a few minutes around 11:00 a.m. to have coffee in turn. British hospitals were always arranged in wards or rooms with a connecting end post or duty room which overlooked the whole scene. One could enjoy a steaming mug of coffee and a chat and still keep an eye on the patients.

As I raised my cup to my lips, someone said to me, "I see there's a posting up on the board for you." I nearly dropped my mug. "Where to?" I asked. She said she thought it was for the Far East and I replied that she must surely be mistaken; if overseas, it was probably the Middle East. At lunchtime I ventured over to the mess and sure enough, there on the board was my name and a notice of my posting to the Far East.

Of course, this was a only short compassionate posting that I was serving at Buckland House, not a home posting. I had known there was a chance of being sent overseas again, and as everything was fine with Mother, there was no reason not to go. VE day did not mean the end of the war, and orders were orders.

"But to the Far East?" I thought. The Far East had never held any special attraction for me. But I couldn't very well go over to the matron and say, "Look, I don't want to go to the Far East, could I just go somewhere else instead?"

I should have expected this, but I was devastated. The first thing I did was to cable Robert, knowing as I sent it that he would be quite upset. Then, I started packing, thinking of the awful things I had heard about the Far East. Maybe the war would end before I got there.

Just after receiving news of the posting I found out that my mother's cousin's son was escaping ahead of the Japanese through the Burma jungle. So at least I would have family over there. He had been a principal of a church school near Rangoon, Burma before the Japanese invasion.

The day before my departure I was called to the matron's office and informed that my Far East posting had been cancelled and that my new posting to the south of England had arrived. I was overjoyed but bewildered. Had someone read my thoughts? I received the explanation later: one Major Aikens had contacted the Canadian section of the War Office in London and requested the posting be stopped because he was about to leave for the U.K. and our wedding. Actually he wasn't scheduled to arrive for four months, but I didn't mind.

There was lots of tea and talking in the mess that night. I still couldn't believe what Robert had done. If anyone had told me that he would proceed to have my posting stopped, I never would have believed it. But there it was. Obviously, there was much I had to learn about this man I was to marry.

Anstie Grange – June 1945

I proceeded to the Q.A. holding unit, Anstie Grange, Homewood Surrey, England, to be Home Sister until I was married. This was a recruiting and mobilizing centre like

Peebles and Tidworth, where nurses were processed after joining the Q.A. Reserves and before being sent overseas. I supposed many of these would be going to the Far East. No one stayed at Anstie Grange for more than a few days.

The mansion had originally belonged to an admiral, but we knew little of the present owner. That the ancestors of this gracious house had been seafaring people was obvious by the portraits and pictures arranged on the walls and the books in the library.

My room was in the attic. It was tiny, bare and cold. It was nice having a room of my own, but not as much fun as sharing with another Sister. Of course, I was rarely in my room except to sleep, because there were lots of other tasks to keep me occupied around the house.

The matron and I met each morning to review the day's procedures. After our meeting, I would go to the kitchen and arrange, with the help of the cook, the day's menu, and then review lists. I had to ensure that there was always enough bedding, towels, toiletries, snacks and meal supplies. I had to check and supervise the cleaning of the whole building and see to the changing of the beds and laundry along with the Army Territorial Service (ATS).

There were some pleasanter chores. If the matron was expecting guests that day, for instance, I would stroll through the garden, carefully cutting the most beautiful and fragrant flowers, and arrange them in the dining rooms and hallways. I also looked after laying the large mahogany table with fine bone china and heavy cutlery. If Matron decided it was warm enough take afternoon tea out of doors, then I would have everything set up on a table in the garden. There was an old, gnarled pine at one corner of the garden, and quite often, because it was shady and cool in that area, I would have the table set up there.

I was expected to join the matron and her guests at these functions, and I enjoyed the pleasant chatter and the surrounding beauty of the grounds. I met such a selection of important military people that I forgot their names after they left; Matron and I would have a chuckle about that. The matron herself was a darling Irishwoman, quite a character, patriotic, a disciplinarian and a devoted Q.A. Regular. We became quite good friends. She was a hard worker and knew how to supervise her workers and keep them strictly in line.

There were no patients here; my duties were completely domestic. Early each morning, I was awakened by the familiar call of an ATS bringing in a cup of tea, a refreshment which seemed to have become a staple for me.

Throughout the war overseas, our 6:00 a.m. tea had been brought to us by batmen who would rattle the cups and say "Wakey, wakey, rise and shine." During the Bari Raid a huge bucket of tea sat beside a hurricane lamp, and an orderly or batman would dish out the warm liquid for us. No "wakey, wakey" then, as none of us had been to bed. Nothing to eat with it, either, and no one politely asking whether milk or sugar was required. The tea had probably been made with hot tapwater, but it kept us awake and warm. Here at Anstie Grange the maid had left the tea outside my door after knocking and calling out the time. There was even a cookie in the saucer and it was a real china cup and saucer at that. No tin cup here.

It was a very busy time for me, working here while trying to arrange a wedding with Mother. Matron wanted me to be married at Anstie Grange – a temptation – but I had promised Mother I would be married in Wales. Matron and the staff were very helpful to me and I will never forget their kindness. I bought my wedding dress from one of the people on staff there and although it wasn't new, it had only been worn once and saved me a lot of money. Mother was arranging things in north Wales for Robert's arrival.

As soon as I had the date settled, I met with the minister to confirm all the details. He made numerous inquiries, some of which I thought were most unnecessary, but I suppose he was doing his job and also thinking of me. A Canadian couldn't just come into England and say, "Here I am, let's get married!' and you couldn't certainly do that in Wales, especially in this old-fashioned church of ours, and during wartime. It wouldn't have surprised me if they had sent for Robert's parents' birth certificates and a recommendation from his army unit. They were very fussy.

North Wales was a long way from Surrey and Anstie Grange. Mother had no phone and without a vehicle I couldn't just drive over, either. I had to help Mother arrange for my bridesmaids' dresses; six of these people were coming from Swansea, my home town, and had never even been to north Wales before. Robert had no relatives in Britain and didn't know anyone here, so we arranged for his best man, Stanley Jones. Stanley was a naval officer on leave at the time. His family and mine had been friends for years; his mother and mine had gone to school together and I had grown up with him and his sister, although I had only seen Stanley on school holidays.

There was time to sit down and relax now and again, amidst the work at the house and the wedding preparations. Matron and I talked about all sorts of things over cups of tea and biscuits. She had at one time served in Candy, Ceylon, now Sri Lanka. We talked how there were so many rules and regulations governing all aspects of army life and I related my encounters with those rules and regulations. Matron said that the army did not take kindly to people having nothing to do in their spare time and it was important to read good books, climb mountains or do whatever else offered.

Matron couldn't understand why I would go to Canada and thought Robert and I would be better off in staying in England or Wales where the weather was pleasant and where my friends and family were. I was beginning to wonder myself how I was going to adjust to it all. I was giving up three loves – my mother, my country and my profession.

Robert Comes to England – October 1945

Robert arrived in London from the Middle East in early October, checked in to a downtown hotel and registered for a medical course which he wanted to take in Hammersmith right after the wedding. Those arrangements and a few others made, he boarded a train for Anstie Grange.

His arrival at the house was a grand affair, with introductions all around. Matron was beaming and happily went about preparing a tasty afternoon lunch during which Robert captured everyone's attention with various anecdotes. In the late afternoon Robert and I left to take the train for Llanasa, north Wales.

After more than a year's separation, it was almost like meeting Robert again for the first time, but we fell into easy conversation on the train, and he kept me amused with reminiscences of our times in Italy. Everyone took an immediate liking to Robert and he and my mother were friends from their first smile and handshake. I always thought they would be, as they both possessed the same kinds of good qualities. I suddenly wondered what Bob's parents would be like.

I had to reprimand myself silently for thinking of my feelings instead of my mother's. After my father had died, my mother had devoted herself to my proper upbringing and had gone to work to support me. And now, I was preparing to leave for another country, maybe for good, and she would be alone. She wouldn't be able to visit at a moment's notice and neither would I.

I wondered if Mother wished she had never broken my first engagement 10 years ago. She had said I was too young and should get an education first. But if I had married the fellow as planned, now Mother would have had my home close by to visit and would likely have grandchildren around her. Instead, two families who had once been close were separated due to the broken engagement, I had been home only once or twice since beginning my nursing training and now I was planning move to a different continent.

I couldn't leave my country without taking some mementoes along. Nestled carefully between the layers of clothing in my suitcase were a number of special snapshots of various places in Britain. Some were of favourite places such as Anstie Grange and Peebles Hydro, and others included familiar faces of many of the girls I had trained and worked with, constant reminders of my time at war.

Although maybe I should have been in uniform because Robert was, my mother would not have liked it. This was to be a pretty wedding and, of course, I had already purchased my wedding dress from one of the girls at Anstie Grange.

The gown was of white satin beaut, with a delicate heart-shaped neckline, 24 tiny pearl buttons down the back and a length of train below them that my train-bearers would carry. The head veil and orange blossom belonged to someone's grandmother, I can't remember whose. I would carry red carnations.

My train-bearers were two charming little girls, Mary and Pamela, one of whom was my cousin. Their delicate dresses were made of soft hues of pink, and their matching floral headdresses were handmade with real flowers.

My favourite cousin Violet from Swansea was one of my matrons of honour. She would wear a long gown of pale blue taffeta and carry Victorian posy. My other matron of honour was Mother's cousin Nesta Jones. She had chosen to wear a long flowing dress made of petunia taffeta and she would also be carrying Victorian posy.

Nesta's husband had been overseas and our paths had crossed once in North Africa. She and her husband lived with Nesta's mother in the little village post office next to the church. Her mother was the current town postmistress; the Jones family had handled the village post for over a hundred years.

The beautiful old stone church tucked away on a lane in the middle of the village of Llanasa had been built around 1372. The interior was resplendent with gleaming solid oak pews. The family of Bob's best man Stanley Jones (different Joneses from Nesta's family) had been vergers of this church for the last century and Stanley's father was the incumbent, so I knew the church would be all dressed up. Actually, the villagers had been busy the night before getting the church ready for Harvest Thanksgiving, which, happily, coincided perfectly with our wedding.

Robert stayed at the Gyrn Arms Hotel, a short walk from the church, while I was at home with Mother. The house in which my mother was staying had belonged at one time to my grandparents. Some friends lived there now and Mother was living there on a temporary basis. Some of the people who had come from Swansea for the wedding were also staying there, so it was full of people.

The house was called Cartref, which was Welsh for "home." It had originally been a schoolhouse and part of a convent called Talacre Abbey.

My mother had been taught by the nuns of that convent. She was not a Roman Catholic, but my grandparents had wanted the best teachers for her and her sister Louise. They had lived in a place called "the Elms" at Gronant, a village on the other side of an immense estate surrounding the Abbey, and later moved to Llanasa.

Cartref was located about four miles from the Gyrn Arms and the distance gave Robert and me an excuse to tour the town or traipse off into the countryside. Robert loved this country and knew that we would come back often, which made my mother happy. She said that if she had a son she would have liked one just like Robert. We couldn't know it at the time, but Robert's mother and mine were to become very good friends.

The Marriage – October 9, 1945

It could not have been a more beautiful morning. The birds were trilling in chorus and the Abbey bells could be heard faintly across the fields. Everyone had left for the church at Llanasa except my mother's cousin Eric, who was giving me away, and me. I got into the carefully prepared car, Eric making sure my train was OK, and the two of us set off, right on time.

Such vivid memories took over my mind as we drove along to the church. When I had visited my grandparents here as a little girl, I had walked this narrow road to church with my family, picking mushrooms along the way.

Suddenly, after we had been on the road for about five minutes my mind jolted me back to the present. "Oh my gosh, Eric," I blurted out, "you've got to get me back to the house fast!" I can still see the quizzical expression on Eric's face. He stopped the car abruptly, turned to face me, muttering under his breath, and asked me if I was quite mad. I guess he thought I had changed my mind about getting married.

Certainly not, but I had left my bouquet on the dining room table. He stepped on the gas and we sped back to the house. I think he was feeling rather badly that he hadn't noticed the bouquet resting on the table.

We arrived back at the house and Eric discovered he had somehow misplaced the keys. The place was all locked up. Remembering how tedious it had been getting into the car, I decided that I didn't want to get out again until we were at the church, so I just sat and waited. Eric jumped out, shouting, "Keep calm!" and disappeared around the back of the house. About ten minutes later, he jogged back to the car, my bouquet in one arm and his jacket on the other. From the beads of sweat on his brow it, looked as if he had just undergone some rigorous exercise. He expressed hope that my mother wouldn't mind the newly broken window. We set off again, no daydreaming this time!!

We weren't too late. There were still a few guests standing about on the steps or in the lobby, chatting and looking towards the wedding car as it pulled up. Upon sighting us, they moved inside to take seats, a few waiting for a glimpse of the bride as I alighted from the car. It was a lovely sunny morning, with no breeze to blow anything out of place.

As I crossed the threshold of the church, I noted that not another person could have squeezed inside. The service itself was a blur – it all happened quickly, and Robert and I were both very nervous. I do remember thinking how beautiful the organ music sounded in the old building. The organ had been there since my grandfather was a young boy, and the church's organist had been playing it ever since I was a child.

Before we knew it, we were on the steps of the church, smiling and surrounded by well-wishers throwing confetti and rice. In those days the bride did not throw her bouquet but instead gave it to the nearest little hospital. I wanted to take mine across the road to the cemetery and place it on the resting spot of my grandparents, but someone advised me that I would probably have the whole village following me into the cemetery so, rather than playing Pied Piper in my wedding gown, I hung on to the bouquet for the moment, delivering it later to the childrens' ward of the hospital.

Morning weddings were quite common in those days in Wales. The wedding breakfast, similar to an afternoon or evening reception, was held at the Gyrn Arms hotel. Just as my mother and the village women had made sure that the wedding would be a very pretty one, they had obviously put in many hours of preparation for the wedding breakfast; the area had been prettily decorated with flowers and leaves and ribbons.

Even though it was breakfast, we still had a wedding cake. My aunt in Bristol had baked it specially and sent it up a few days ago. She was not able to attend the wedding, but we would be visiting her in Bristol and would give her all the details and compliment her on the cake.

There were twelve or fourteen of us seated around the table, mostly close relatives. A friend of Mother's from Prestatyn made one speech and Stanley made the other one, making us all laugh with comments on the difficulties we had all been through to get there.

We left the Gyrn Arms in a borrowed car. It wasn't decorated, but trailing along the back, as we discovered shortly, were two large tin cans which made an awful clatter as we pulled away from the church. To the back bumper was attached a large piece of cardboard on which someone had drawn a maple leaf for Canada and a daffodil for Wales. The inscription underneath was "Canada Forever" and "Cymru am Byth," which in Welsh means "Wales Forever." We decided that Stanley had been the one behind the cans and the card.

As we settled ourselves in the train carriage I remember Robert trying his best to brush all the confetti off me. The surrounding passengers were grinning at the scene because Robert himself was absolutely covered with confetti. He was so easily embarrassed that it was difficult at that moment to imagine him in El Alamein looking after the troops of the Eighth Army.

We spent our honeymoon at Marlow on the Thames in the George and Dragon Hotel. When we were registering, the manager said, "Good morning, I'm George, the dragon is upstairs." The manager's friendliness was an indication of the atmosphere in his hotel.

Such a delightful spot was Marlow. We went rowing on the Thames. It was funny getting back in a boat, and it seemed a long time since the Strathallan and those crowded lifeboats. The hotel supplied the London Times and The

Telegraph newspapers and we followed the progress towards the definitive end to the war and worked the papers' crossword puzzles in the evenings. For me this was continuation of a family tradition, and I had seen Bob doing the crosswords on the ambulance train.

Marlow was just a short distance from London. Robert had spent some time in London during the blackout and had been amazed at how the crowds and busy traffic could get through successfully without any street lights.

We looked for accommodation in London for when Robert was taking his course in Hammersmith, and soon chose Inverness Terrace in Bayswater. We were to have one room and would share a bathroom. We weren't keen on that arrangement but accommodation was difficult to come by then and we didn't have very much money.

We were both sending money home, Bob to his parents to help pay for his younger brother's university tuition and I to my mother to help her out. We realized that it would be tough going in Canada while he studied for his fellowship in medicine and before he started a practice.

There was lots of work for staff nurses in London and I knew that I would have no difficulty at all, with my training and experience, getting a job in one of the hospitals nearby. Robert was very much against me working, but our circumstances didn't leave us with a choice.

We walked for miles around London, around the banks of the Serpentine River, through Hyde Park and the beauty of Kensington Gardens. We utilized the underground railway to get to places we couldn't reach on foot. We splurged on theatre many times. Robert knew I liked Ivor Novello, the Welsh playwright, so we went to see a performance called "Perchance to Dream" in which he sang. As Robert liked the music of Grieg, we also went to see "A Song of Norway."

Try as I might, however, I couldn't convince Robert of the beauty of ballet, though I convinced him to take in one performance. He was so funny afterwards. He could see no reason at all for this man in tights to be carrying a perfectly healthy girl in a short skirt back and forth across the stage. But the music won him over, he had to admit, and so we bought some of the music from the ballet but didn't go to any more performances after that.

We talked endlessly about the war and hospitals and all the things we wanted to accomplish. I am sure I could have persuaded him to stay in London permanently at that time, as he got along so well with all the officers and also because there were so many opportunities for higher education there. But he was always talking about this Dalhousie University in Halifax and how he might have priority there as a native Nova Scotian, so I decided not to pursue the issue. I would dearly have loved to stay on in England, but I knew that this fiercely determined man would complete his fellowship of the Royal College where he thought it best and that it would probably be back in Canada.

Throughout our most serious discussions we maintained our good sense of humour, one of the things that had attracted us to each other in the first place. We enjoyed many moments of hilarity over some silly incident or upon reading a certain passage in a book or paper.

We also both liked sports, although we had been exposed to different ones. Robert had played some hockey in university, although, as he said, it wasn't really a social game and one couldn't call up a friend for a game of hockey. He was interested in sports like cricket which were new to him and would cheerfully accompany me to watch it.

Our army training had enabled us rise early and make the most of each day, but our five days in Marlow vanished all too soon. Our bill from the George and Dragon was meticulously itemized. It seemed as though the proprietors had known everything about us from what we ate in the morning for breakfast to what time we had taken a bath! We found it so funny. We supposed it was because these were all paid items, even the bath, and war rationing would account for much of this practice.

I told Robert that when I was in Sheffield our baths had a black line painted around the lower twelve inches and above that line bathwater did not go. We had called it the Plimsoll line, the line on the side of a ship to show the limit of legal submersion under various conditions. We thought that quite appropriate to the bathing situation too!

Back on Duty – Late

After the honeymoon Robert remained in London to study and I now had to report to London. However, I didn't know to where I was supposed report. I figured that, even though I was so used to waiting for instructions, that I had better make some inquiries about the army's plans for me. Perhaps I should be applying for my release from the army? Upon arriving home to north Wales I found a cable awaiting me. No one had known where Robert and I had gone on our honeymoon, so Mother had held on to it for me.

The cable directed me to report to the hospital at Shrewsbury on a date which by now had passed. I left the next day but was four days late at the hospital. Upon arriving, I was advised that I was in serious trouble as I had been technically AWOL, or absent without leave, and that meant a court-martial. "Surely they wouldn't do that to a new bride?" I naively thought. It wasn't as if I hadn't shown up at all. But the reality of the situation was that I was an officer of the army and I was to be treated like one.

The hospital was a very formal one. I was assigned to the officers' ward, to look after officers who had been sent home from North Africa and Italy with serious injuries. The hospital was extremely busy, but it was much better staffed than many of the places I had been.

Shrewsbury was a nice old city that had escaped bombing, but the hospital was far out of town and transportation was difficult. On my off time I walked the countryside and wrote numerous letters to my new husband.

Court-martialled

Exactly one week after arriving at the hospital in Shrewsbury, I was told to be at the matron's office at 6:00 sharp the next evening in complete service uniform. From there I would be escorted to the Shrewsbury Assizes.

So this was my payment for being a little late! I did not sleep that night and decided not to tell Robert about this little run-in with the law, as he was in London starting his course and I didn't want to worry him or distract him from his studies.

The Shrewsbury Assizes I knew nothing about, but I remembered that when we were overseas a court-martial sounded like a terrible thing to have to go through. I felt apprehensive and alone. I didn't know anyone in this whole place. Our lecturers at the Hydro in Peebles had warned us that if we were captured and interrogated, we must not cry. They hadn't covered what to do if you were court-martialled for returning late from your honeymoon!

I was downstairs in my service uniform at the specified time the next evening, and felt quite brave until I came face to face with the two guards who were to escort me. They led me outside to the army van, and my legs were shaking as I realized that these people meant business.

It was humiliating to have everyone watching from the windows above, speculating as to what I had done. I wonder if they ever heard about it at Buckland House – news often travelled more quickly than anything else!

Not a word was spoken all the way into Shrewsbury. The van was armed, and I guess the guards driving it and escorting me were also armed, as they were in full dress uniform. We looked rather smart – all dressed up for my execution, or that's what I was beginning to think.

There were more guards at the entrance to the Assizes when we arrived. Did they think I was going to jump out and shoot someone? At the top of the steps I was met by another officer who escorted me to a dark, gloomy anteroom where I was to wait with yet another officer. My fear was quickly being replaced by anger! At least the officer sitting with me was enough of a human being actually to speak to me. His wife was a Q.A. Reserve as well.

He asked me if I knew anything about the "King's Regs" (Regulations) and I answered that I didn't, but all I had done was to return four days late from my honeymoon. I asked him why the powers that be hadn't done the most practical thing and given me the posting when I left Anstie Grange. "They did not even send the cable to the right address," I explained to him. He did seem upset by this news, and I was now so angry that I was trembling like a leaf.

I was finally ushered into a very bright room. Bright lights, dazzling brass, red ribbon, royal crests, a large painting of George VI on the wall, black leather and polished wood – overwhelming. In the big chair was the "top brass," with an officer seated at each side and me centred before them, standing. What I guess were the King's Regs were read; they droned on monotonously, and I was tired and did not understand what they meant.

"And you deliberately stayed away for four days without permission or leave," he said. I heard that alright and replied tartly, "Actually, I almost did not come back."

"Now you're being flippant, Sister," he said. That comment took me from anger to fury. I told him that the telegram delivered to my mother was wrongly addressed and that I might never have received the proper notification.

I assumed they thought I was making excuses. I tried to explain to them how difficult it was to receive mail in that remote area of Wales, especially if the address was incorrect. I really wasn't supposed to speak, but the word "flippant" had made me so mad I could not stop. "I joined the army to nurse the patients, not to play tennis or get court-martialled!" (This in reference to my original Q.A. interview, in which my tennis ability had been an issue.)

I think he found my dissertation amusing, and after a few words of encouragement and gentle reprimand I was escorted out. One would have thought I had been involved in a dastardly espionage plot, not a honeymoon!

And the sentence handed down by the Assizes? I was posted back to the hospital for two weeks and then – into the *custody* of my husband until my demobilization came through! I was not amused at the time. But Robert found it very funny, especially the bit about the tennis, and I finally gave in to the humour of it all.

My brief stay at the hospital unit in Shrewsbury was unpleasant. The matron there prepared a letter of apology to the matron-in-chief in London for me to copy over in my own handwriting. I refused to write anything remotely resembling what it said. It gave no explanation and concluded with, "I beg to have the honour to remain your most humble and obedient servant." I wrote my own letter of apology, mailed it promptly and, when my "sentence" was over, left happily for London and the custody of Robert.

London – January 1946

Our little room in London was working out alright and I had found a temporary job in a nearby hospital. But the best news of all was that we were going to have a baby. We were so thrilled and mother was terribly excited. Robert was leaving for Canada in two months and I could now spend some time with Mother in north Wales while looking forward to our first arrival.

I was released from the army on January 22, 1946. On February 5 I was in the Samaritan Hospital in London and had lost my baby.

It was a sad day for me when Robert left me on the first day of April 1946, but he had to be demobilized in Canada and I would stay in Wales until the Canadian authorities arranged for me to join him. Robert knew how I felt and with his usual reassurance told me that according to Greek mythology his namesake Leander had swum the Hellespont to rescue his lady fair. I didn't know much about Greek mythology but I believed him when he said we were always meant to be together and I would join him in Canada very soon.

EPILOGUE
Return to Bari, Italy, 1995

In 1995 I was invited to go with my son and his family to Corfu for a holiday. It was an offer I couldn't refuse, even though I had to look up Corfu on the map.

After arriving in Corfu, I realized that the port of Corfu was close to Bari and that a ferry ran across. We arranged an overnight ferry booking to visit the area where Robert and I met in World War II and the British War Cemetery.

I was up at 6:30 as usual on the morning of our arrival. I quietly got dressed and sat on deck to gaze at the sea and think my thoughts as the coast of Italy came into view. Language was a barrier in Bari, but eventually we arranged a taxi to drive us to the war cemetery and to return us to dockside.

Here I was after 50 years in a city I had never seen before – new modern buildings, new roads, everyone in civilian clothes, even the traffic c was going too fast.

We were soon at the entrance to the British War Cemetery – it was well kept, with flowers and trees everywhere. I walked among the headstones. Most of these men were so young and here I was almost 80. As the poem goes,

> They shall not grow old
> as we who are left grow old–
> *age shall not weary them*

I took a few pictures; the names didn't mean a thing to me any more, but dates I could identify with. I took a picture of one headstone of a soldier of 24, who had died on Christmas Day, 1943. A patient of mine had died on that day – was this his grave?

I thought there would be a lot of men from the Bari Raid – from December 2, 1943 and the several days after – but there were none! Maybe the cemetery hadn't been established at that time, but then where were those men? And how, then, had the Christmas Day headstone gotten in here? Easily 1000 dead, more like 2000, and there was not even a memorial.

It had been kept a secret for 50 years, but those brave men from many countries fighting for the freedom of others, they must never be forgotten. They weren't to know that wars never solve anything.

Before leaving the cemetery I found the visitors' book to sign. It was obvious that many people came to visit. I glanced through the pages to see if there were any from the UK – people I had worked with, but the tears came as I saw "God bless you, my son" from a mother. I closed the book and placed it gently in the special alcove in the wall and we left.

The taxi took us back to the dockside through an old part of the city. I wondered where the huge military hospital complex had been.

We passed an old abandoned building with torn theatre notices stuck on the walls. Was that where Robert and I had gone to see Irving Berlin and the U.S. troops doing a musical show in 1944?

Further along the same road we saw a large old railway station, slightly familiar; it could have been where we arrived with the ambulance trains and transferred the patients to waiting ambulances for the rest of their journey to the 98th General Base Hospital before heading off for a bath and a good meal and rest between runs up the coast.

We arrived back at the Bari docks and boarded the ferry. I looked down at the docks and the people milling about. The area was large, new and modern. Probably because of lack of money, it would not have been rebuilt for some time after World War II.

I looked down at the calm blue water and it became almost transparent as I imagined over 17 sunken ships, and troops and crews who had not been able to get away, along with citizens of Bari, all of whom had felt safe that night, now that the fighting had moved further up the coast.

Robert and I had always planned to visit Italy in our retirement. There had never been enough money before his early death in 1972. I was pleased to have had the opportunity to visit here with my son and his family, but quite ready to leave for all time.

[This story appeared in the London Daily Express during World War II. Miss Mac was a Q.A. Reserve whom I knew, although we never worked together. – G.A.]

'She blushed faster than any woman we knew'

SALUTE THE SISTER

This story, date-lined Naples, about an English girl who nursed the Americans Italy, is written by Newbold Noyes jun., son of the owner of the Washington Star, and is reprinted in the Daily Express by permission.

We stood with our hats off and thought about Sister Mac. We had not seen her for a couple of months, but the days when she took care of us in Ward 4D East, in the British General Hospital in Naples seemed very close this afternoon. A pale, slender girl, with dark hair and eyes, she was very conscious of the two pips on her shoulder.

The British call their nurses "Sister," but it is not a term of familiarity.

Miss Mac liked discipline and order. That was why she had such a hard time with Ward 4, where American Field Service volunteer ambulance drivers stayed when they were sick.

We were unruly, untidy and sometimes a little impolite, which she could not understand at all. Some of us were there long enough to get to know her pretty well.

"THE DEAN"

Bernie, who had been in bed for six weeks, was "Dean" of the ward. I was there nearly as long. The atmosphere of the place was that of a club, and chief business was teasing Miss Mac.

We never called her by her real name. Sometimes we called her "Beautiful," which made her blush quickest of all.

That was a remarkable thing about Miss Mac – she blushed faster and more violently than any woman we ever saw. It became a game with us. Somebody would compliment her on her hairdo, or ask her if she had a date that night, or refer to her as "The Dean's Girl," and immediately her skin would glow like a cloud with the sun rising behind it.

Her worst days were those on which the colonel inspected the wards. She could not believe that Wally could really want to light a cigar just at the crucial moment. She would rush about opening windows and getting the smoke out of the room.

CHRISTMAS EVE

On Christmas Eve somebody got hold of a bottle of brandy. We made milk punch in a hospital bucket, and lured her in for the party.

One of the boys had received a Christmas stocking from home, and ...we turned it into a present for Miss Mac. We put in some cigarettes, candy, a cake of toilet soap, and a little jar of cleansing cream, which somebody had been carrying around. Wally put in one of his cigars, and we filled up the rest with oranges and nuts.

That day, when she opened her drawer there it was, bulging and red, with a card saying, "Merry Christmas, Miss Mac."

She picked it up and turned slowly to face us, the blood rushing to the roots of her hair. She opened her mouth just once, but nothing came out, and then she ran from the room.

But when she came back her hand was specially gentle as she took our pulses, and tucked in the sheets.

SALUTE

That was about three months ago.

The day before yesterday the Germans raided Naples, and bombs fell on the hospital.

So this afternoon those of us who could get there stood with our hats off and thought about Miss Mac. Her coffin looked incredibly small as they lowered it into the ground.

At the end, all the officers of the hospital stood one by one before her grave and saluted. You could not help thinking how that would have made her blush.

"The Dean" cried more than the rest of us, which was only natural, because she had taken care of him the longest.